A PARENTING INSTRUCTION MANUAL

**Biblically Based
Child Psychiatrist Authored**

by

Dan A. Myers, M.D.

TABLE OF CONTENTS

ACKNOWLEDGEMENTS 1
PREFACE 3
PART I
PARENTING MESSAGES FROM THE OLD TESTAMENT 7
   INTRODUCTION 9
   CHAPTER ONE
      THE BIBLE AS A CHILD-REARING MANUAL 13
   CHAPTER TWO
      THE GENES IN THE JEANS 17
   CHAPTER THREE
      THE IMPORTANT FIRST FIVE YEARS 23
   CHAPTER FOUR
      PRAYER WITH YOUNG CHILDREN 31
   CHAPTER FIVE
      PARENTS: MESSENGERS FOR GOD'S LOVE 37
   CHAPTER SIX
      WHAT IS "QUALITY TIME?" 43
   CHAPTER SEVEN
      CHILDREN ARE NOT LIKE THEY USED TO BE 55
   CHAPTER EIGHT
      GIVING YOUR CHILD A GOOD AND LONG LIFE .. 61
   CHAPTER NINE
      DISCIPLINE AS LOVE 71
   CHAPTER TEN
      EDUCATION IS NOT THE ANSWER 79
   CHAPTER ELEVEN
      THE PERILS OF WEALTH 85
   CHAPTER TWELVE
      SABOTAGING PARENTING WITH SLEEPOVERS ... 95
   CHAPTER THIRTEEN
      DIVORCE AND CHILD CUSTODY 101
   PART I - SUMMING UP 109

PART II
PARENTING MESSAGES FROM THE NEW TESTAMENT ... 111

INTRODUCTION ... 113

CHAPTER ONE
KEEPING THINGS IN PERSPECTIVE: ... 115

CHAPTER TWO
WHAT A FRIEND WE HAVE IN JESUS ... 119

CHAPTER THREE
WHO WAS JESUS? ... 123

CHAPTER FOUR
WHAT WAS JESUS LIKE? ... 125

CHAPTER FIVE
DAN'S LIST OF OTHER CHARACTERISTICS OF CHRIST ... 133

CHAPTER SIX
A CHRISTIAN MISCONCEPTION ... 145

CHAPTER SEVEN
WHEN YOUR CHILD NEEDS A PSYCHIATRIST? ... 151

CHAPTER EIGHT
MYTHS ABOUT PSYCHOACTIVE MEDICATIONS ... 155

CHAPTER NINE
SENDING YOUR CHILD TO COLLEGE ... 159

CHAPTER TEN
PARENT PRAYING ... 169

PART II - SUMMING UP ... 173
NOTES ... 175

Dedicated

to my wife
Kathy Nerger Hawn Myers

to our children
Simone Myers Howell
Yvette Myers Thompson
Belen Myers Linton
Heather Hawn Roberts
Lacy Hawn Schult
Dan Myers Jr.

to our grandchildren
Daniel Howell Jolley
Barret Howell
Rock Linton
Boone Howell
Margot Linton
Dylan Myers Thompson
Katie Myers
Kathleen Hawn Roberts
Ella Myers
Sarah Hawn Roberts
Gretchen Hawn Schultz
Courtney Hawn Schultz
Annie Myers

to our great grandchild
John Jolley IV

ACKNOWLEDGEMENTS

My interest and understanding of Scripture has for over thirty years been stoked by the Poole/Hundley Bible Study at Highland Park Presbyterian Church in Dallas Texas. Nowhere have I felt the Holy Spirit as intensely present as during the discussion, laughter, interpretation and application of Scripture that occurs during the weekly sessions with these Christian men. I can't imagine that I could have written this book or even stayed a Christian without them.

Proceeds from the sale of this book will go to the Highland Park Presbyterian Church Rainey Day Fund with the understanding that if members of the Hundley/Poole Bible Study have emergency financial needs, they will be given some preference for funds that have been collected from the sale of this book.

Copyright © 2020 by Dan A. Myers MD
Scripture quotes are from The New International Version of the Bible

PREFACE

My first book, <u>Golden Rules for Parenting, A Child Psychiatrist Discovers the Bible</u>, was published by the Paulist Press in 1999. The book largely was a result of my 20-year marriage with four children ending in a messy divorce, followed by seven years of bachelorhood characterized by excessing working, running marathons, drinking, gambling, and dating, all which ultimately waned after meeting Kathy Hawn and marrying her and her two young daughters in 1984. How, fifteen years later, I could become known as a "Church Guy" and to have self-published four religious books, God only knows. Details of the wilder period of my life are self-published and available on Amazon.com, <u>The Book of Dan, 79 Years To Redemption</u>. It is more entertaining than what you are about to read, but I doubt it will do you near as much good.

After marrying Kathy, my son Dan Jr., who was the same age as 11 year old Lacy and two years younger than 13 year old Heather, came into our custody. We began to go to Church together as a family. While listening to a sermon one Sunday, the thought came to me that, although reading historical fiction had been a passion, I had never read the account of Jesus in the Bible (in those days I thought the New Testament was historical fiction). That evening I opened a Bible Kathy's sister had given to me for Christmas (hint, hint) and started reading in the book of Matthew.

In my practice of child psychiatry, I began to notice that the parents of the children who seemed to be managing and enjoying their children best were living Christian lives.

At the time, I was attempting to write a secular parenting manual. However, I was frustrated by having difficulty choosing which child-rearing issues to include. Surprisingly, even to me, I decided to let my new Bible reading project be my guide. Systematically, I started at Genesis and worked through the entire Bible, comparing its parenting instructions with what I had learned as a child psychiatrist. Everything that I wrote was at least provoked by Bible reading. In the process, my growing Christian faith increased, so by the time <u>Golden Rules For Parenting</u> was published, I had become a Christian.

Suddenly my thoughts during most of my waking moments became theology-oriented, and my private prayer life greatly increased. These phenomena were so unfamiliar and foreign that I consulted both an expert psychiatrist (I knew many) and a minister (I knew one). The psychiatrist said I did not have a "disorder." The minister explained this change was called "being born again," that "walking from darkness into light" had been a shock.

After <u>Golden Rules For Parenting</u> (now out of print), I self-published two other books on Biblical parenting and lectured on this topic in Cuba, Romania and China. Writing and lecturing gave me the unique gift of being able to inform my grown children of Biblical principles they had missed growing up with a father who was not a Christian leader in the home.

Over the next twenty years as I became more mature in my Christian faith, had more experience as a psychiatrist and as a parent. I saw the immense benefit of the Bible for childrearing guidance. My career as a child psychiatrist kept me aware of modern views about child rearing. Through fifty years of practicing child psychiatry, I evaluated children and parents; some who were practicing the best and some the worst parenting. My first 20 years of practicing psychiatry was as a heathen, compared with the last 30 years as a strong Christian: Life, and my practice, were better as a Christian!

My life experience as a parent is extensive. Three outstanding daughters and one outstanding son resulted from a first marriage lasting 20 years. I have weathered a difficult divorce and put together and enjoyed a blended family for thirty-four years. All of our children and stepchildren have graduated from college, had traditional Christian weddings and all are financially independent. Please pardon me if this seem to be bragging. Muhammad Ali said, "It is not bragging, if it's true."

Of course, this great parenting result came about for many other reasons than me being such a skillful father. However, I should at least get a little credit that I didn't mess things up. I am now 82 years old. If I don't share all this experience by putting it into a <u>Parenting Instruction Manual</u> before I die, it would be a real waste.

Please use your commonsense in deciding the reasonableness of my conclusions and recommendations. Looking up the Bible quotes and reading their background is encouraged, as for brevity's sake most are taken out of context. I ask the same for my writing. By trying to be as straightforward as possible, my instructions, particularly if they are taken out of context, may seem more dogmatic than was my intent.

Because I realize, ten years later, that my first book, <u>Golden Rules For Parenting</u>, was almost exclusively derived from Old Testament Scripture, this book is divided into two parts. Rereading the New Testament as a more mature Christian opened up much more new parenting instruction material. This made it logical to piggyback my new findings onto a rewritten version of the material from <u>Golden Rules For Parenting</u>. This does not mean there is a known advantage for a parent to categorize instruction into "New" or "Old Testament." This is just happens to be the way the Holy Spirit laid it out to me.

PART I

PARENTING MESSAGES FROM THE OLD TESTAMENT

Parenting Messages from the Old Testament is particularly relevant for parents with younger children and contains many practical, child-rearing techniques. Its focus is on rearing children who will live civilized and productive lives on earth. Instructions in the Old Testament pave the way for accepting what Jesus teaches in the New.

INTRODUCTION

How many times have you heard or thought, "I wish this baby had come with an instruction manual?" Well, this may be that manual. Even though my parenting experience is influenced from practicing fifty years as a child psychiatrist, I am confident that what I have written is consistent with Biblical teaching. I assure you that nothing recommended in the manual is clearly opposed to Biblical instruction. This can be easily verified by checking what is written in the manual against what the Bible says. The big question is whether you believe the Bible.

It is hard to know if you believe the Bible if you have never read it. I first read the Bible when I was 54 years old, a hardened scientific thinker, who never thought he would believe what's in the Bible. Here are a few things that turned my thinking around:

Understanding when people say that the Bible is the "Word of God" means that it is "inerrant." It does not mean that every thing the Bible says is literally correct. It means that nothing in the Bible is a mistake or wrong. God put it there for a reason. Some things that may not seem relevant to us may be perfectly clear to someone in a different culture or time period. One pastor made this suggestion, "Read the Bible like eating a fish. If you find a bone, put it to the side of your plate. Don't throw away the whole fish."

Can you imagine writing text that would be beneficially applied for thousands of cultures over a 4,000 year time period? The Old Testament was written during an age of lawlessness and violence. Commandments, rules and punishments that were necessary to civilize and control these socially primitive people would not be necessary or appropriate for earth's inhabitants in the 21st century. Few of us today would agree or obey a law that said adulterers, fortune tellers and teenagers who have cursed their parents should be killed by stoning. Our common sense and the Jesus of the New Testament modify such radical punishment into something like, "These are serious transgressions and have serious consequences." The prohibition stays in effect; the punishments have been modified.

Being in a Bible study with other trustworthy Christians can help to reach the most accurate interpretations of Scripture. I don't interpret the Adam and Eve story literally, but as a metaphor that may be the closest God could come to expressing his actions so that humans from different eras understand that He is the Creator of our universe and all life forms. For God to explain His creations using scientific principles such as quantum physics would be incomprehensible to the Israelites with Moses in the desert and to most of us today. God will clarify this and other questions for us in Heaven.

To get the most out of the Bible it is important to call upon the Holy Spirit as Jesus directed. The Bible says in John 14:26, that after Jesus rose into Heaven, God sent the Holy Spirit to remain on earth to expand on all the things Jesus had said. Saying a simple, silent prayer, something like the following, will make your Bible study more productive: "Holy Spirit, please help me get the most out of my reading the Bible. Thank you. Amen." A simple prayer like this can be a forerunner of future communication with God. Another way to think of it is that reading the Bible requires a password. That password is a prayer to the Holy Spirit before we begin.

Whichever way you look at it, if you are a Christian you need to read the Bible. Thinking that reading the Bible would be similar to reading an encyclopedia, I was surprised it was so short. The Gospels, the first four books of the New Testament containing almost all (some information is in the Book of Acts) that is known about Jesus' life while He was on earth, are only 146 pages.

The entire New Testament, which chronicles Jesus' life on earth and the early history of the Christian Church, is only

322 pages. For comparison, the first Harry Potter novel, *The Sorcerer's Stone*, is 399 pages. I know young children who have read this book five or six times. Although there have been thousands of commentaries written about Jesus' life, the source of all of them is the same 146 pages. For me, regularly facing the challenge of keeping abreast of reams of medical and psychiatric information, it is refreshing to find that by simply becoming knowledgeable about 146 pages, I can critically evaluate what any expert or preacher proclaims about Jesus. More importantly, reading these 146 pages provides everything needed to decide whether to accept or reject Christ's gift of eternal life.

The Old Testament, a sacred text for both Jews and Christians, records God's laws, describing punishments for disobedience and rewards for obeying. Prophets, humans through whom God spoke, wrote the information in the Old Testament. The 39 books of the Old Testament tell stories of people and nations who have either followed or disobeyed God's instructions. Most of the stories (books) have lessons, morals and instructions that, if you use common sense, are readily applied to modern-day life. In addition, scattered through the Old Testament are prophecies telling of the coming of a Messiah. These prophecies, written 1500 to 500 years before Christ was born, were fulfilled by Christ when he lived and died on earth. Seeing the accuracy of these prophecies as I read the Gospels convinced me that the Bible is God's word.

The Old Testament is 1053 pages in length. That's long, but not much more than Larry McMurtry's book, *Lonesome Dove*, which is 945 pages. The entire Bible, Old Testament plus New Testament, is 1373 pages.

I was proud of myself when I completed reading the Bible. I had personally known few people who had read the Bible cover to cover. However, at that time, I had not been associating with many people who gave reading the Bible a high priority. Reading the Bible can change your life, and it will help you to be a better parent.

Using the Bible as my guide for writing a book on child rearing allowed a safe course. Parents have used its teachings for 4000 years. Child psychiatry has existed as a medical specialty only since 1957, and its theories are regularly being challenged and updated.

There are instructions in the Bible for parents, but they are not grouped together conveniently in a particular book or chapter. <u>A Parenting Instruction Manual</u> sorts out most of the child references for you. That they are scattered throughout Scripture may have been to give us an incentive to read the entire Bible. Also, God may be directing us to put childhood in perspective. Like the flight attendant who tells us to put the oxygen mask on ourselves before helping our children, God may be teaching parents to first make their own lives comply with His Word and then teach their children.

Regular Bible reading and a Bible study group changed the way I think about the Bible. My previous views about the Bible embarrass me. I thought it was a book used by people who were naïve and/or less intelligent. How could I have dismissed as irrelevant a book that has been accepted by billions of people for 2000 years as their life-guide, when I had never even read it?

As I read the Bible, I found that good parenting advice, which I had assumed was modern or original, had been recorded in the Bible thousands of years ago.

I came to appreciate that living with no spiritual guidance handicaps families. Conveying to my grown children the good news of the Bible and how it can be used as a parenting instruction manual was a strong motivation for writing this book. The best thing my Manual could do would be to get you to read the Bible, and the worse thing it could do is to cause you to use the manual instead of reading the Bible. Although this manual has useful tips for child rearing, the most reliable assurance of successful child rearing is to have parents who live Christian lives.

CHAPTER ONE

THE BIBLE AS A CHILD-REARING MANUAL

WHAT THE BIBLE SAYS ABOUT JESUS' PARENTS

During the time of Christ, angels sometimes spoke to humans. For example, an angel told Mary she would become pregnant, being conceived by the Holy Spirit, and would have a son whom she should name "Jesus" (Luke 1:26). Surprisingly, nowhere in the New Testament does it say God or His angels spoke to Mary and Joseph to give them child-rearing instruction for Jesus. Mary and Joseph must have possessed remarkable parenting abilities in order to rear a Messiah without specific direction from God.

Mary and Joseph shared a value system based on the word of God. They implemented their religious Jewish heritage in parenting Jesus. Their parenting instructions came from God through Scripture. The same wisdom is accessible to parents today through reading the Old Testament. In addition, in the New Testament we have the benefit of the teachings of Jesus Christ.

USING THE BIBLE IN MODERN TIMES

Neither the Old nor New Testament is written like a "How To" book on parenting. The Bible seldom gives instructions for specific life situations. Biblical directions are not rigid. Neither the Bible, nor life, is always black or white.

Parents are regularly confronted by situations that come in shades of gray. For example, how are parents able to judge which television shows should be off limits for children and when should restrictions be lifted as the children become more mature? It is difficult. However, if the parents' belief system includes moral standards as described throughout the Bible, countless judgments they will make on behalf of their children will be positively influenced.

It is not possible to completely screen children from all the immorality in our world. However, regular exposure of children to immorality does not better prepare them for adulthood. Their homes should be havens where they can grow and strengthen with a minimum of noxious influences. The more fixed children become in their value system, the better they can withstand and navigate through an immoral adult world.

A psychiatry professor explained it this way: Suppose a man has a job where every day he is ridiculed and humiliated by his boss. Do you think that, to prepare him for work, his wife should hit, curse and snub him at home? No, he needs respite from the cruelty and harshness. The confusion and immorality we too often see in our world does not mean that protecting our children through Biblical direction is irrelevant; it causes us to need the Bible more!

Most psychiatrists have been trained not to intrude into their patients' religious lives. Unfortunately, when the psychiatrist whom the patient trusts and respects does not even mention religion, the patient may assume the psychiatrist sees religious convictions as having no value. This may inadvertently cause the patient to ignore or abandon religious beliefs for psychological theories proposed by the therapist. Ironically, the psychiatrist may be relying on religious guidelines for the good mental health of his or her own family.

When someone needs treatment for emotional problems, it might be ideal to use a devout and scholarly clergyman also trained as a psychiatrist. However, the time-consuming training required for both professions makes this impractical. It appears the best option is to put your faith in the Word of God, and then seek professional assistance if you need it.

Whether a child safely navigates the dangers of growing up is determined by many factors. Some children seem born more flexible, resilient and adaptable than others. Although our interaction with our children can modify their behavior, sometimes the outcome may be largely predetermined by their genetic makeup.

CHAPTER TWO

THE GENES IN THE JEANS

Whether nature (heredity) or nurture (environment) determines personality has been debated for centuries. Some people strongly believe the environment, willpower and effort shape what we become. Others feel our ancestors' genes have set our life's course. There is a religious analogy to this argument. Some Christians strongly believe God gives us free choice. Others emphasize God has our life already planned or predestined. Most scientists conclude both heredity and environment shape us. Most theologians agree God does have a plan for our lives but also permits some free will. These questions have practical implications for parents when they set standards for their children. The difficulty comes in distinguishing what can be changed and what cannot.

What can parents expect from a child? What fundamental strengths has he or she been born with? Do children have weaknesses that cannot be overcome? Which of their characteristics have been inherited, which have been learned and which have been shaped by their environment? The answers to these questions may be the keys to opening doors for a child's success.

ADOPTION

One interesting way to compare heredity with environment is by studying identical twins that have been adopted into different homes. It is remarkable to see how personality traits and behavioral patterns of twins remain similar despite growing up in very different environments. The results of such studies are fascinating and leave no doubt that heredity plays a major role in whom we become. However, the conclusions have limited value for parents predicting height, build, intelligence, artistic ability and physical coordination of an individual child. Statistics are relevant, but are not one hundred percent valid. A particular child may not fit the pattern exhibited by the majority in a study group. More importantly, statistics don't take into consideration the strength of a child's will, the parents management skills or the power of prayer.

Parents with biological children could learn from parents who adopt. Although most parents prefer to have children from their own genetic pool, for the child, adoption could open opportunities and happiness that would have otherwise been impossible. Adopting a child can be a loving and selfless act. Some parents deliberately adopt emotionally damaged, physically or intellectually inferior children to give them a healing home and family life. These parents seem to exemplify God's love, just as He adopted us knowing our faults, sinful nature, and weaknesses. St. Paul writes in Galatians 4:5-7 and Ephesians 1:5, about how we have been adopted into God's family by Christ dying for us. We have become His very own children and may speak of God as "Father." Many parents accept their adoptive children as God created them, seeing themselves as nurturers to guide children to their full potential. They do not try to make their child into what they expect or wish he or she could be.

Most adopting parents work to discover their child's innate abilities, as they know their child does not share their genetic makeup. However, when parents adopt children and then deny the significance of the children's heredity, the results can be unfortunate. It is not possible for children to be something they are not. Children will sense it if they are a disappointment to their parents. When children get older, dissatisfaction and conflict can become more overt.

Such conflict may culminate when a child becomes a teenager. An unhappy, adopted child may abandon the effort of working out his or her problems for the fantasy that "things would have been different if I had my real parents." Parents of a depressed, angry, impulsive, defiant teenager may also want to deny that the child is their responsibility. When the child is adopted, it makes this denial more plausible.

Such scenarios are rare. Most parents find raising an adopted child as satisfying and fulfilling as having a biological child. Many households are made up of a gratifying mix of adopted and biological children. Raising an adopted child should require no different methods than those used with biological children.

However, it is important for adoptive parents to recognize their child will be less like them than if he or she was biologically related. Personality traits, as well as specific physical characteristics, often can be traced through many generations. Behaviors may be learned or taught, but temperament and some personality traits are inherited. Loving and emotionally strong parents may be able to modify and redirect an adopted child's personality, but it may be more of a struggle than the parents anticipated.

The foregoing discussion is to remind adopting parents there will be things about their child that they cannot change. The child, to some degree, will come with his or her own preprogrammed, predestined direction. Most adopting parents already know this. Biological parents may be not as aware that they can face the same issue. Chance, or divine planning, determines which genes we receive. I have seen children who, because of heredity, remain incorrigible despite dedicated skillful, loving, natural parents. There are families where a natural child has psychiatric problems, while the adopted brother or sister is high achieving and emotionally stable. There is no way to foresee which of the millions of genetic combinations for physical and personality traits a particular child will receive. Each child born to natural parents has a chance of being as unfamiliar and different as a child who is adopted. Parents are sometimes heard to say as they observe behaviors of their child, "Where did he or she come from?" Biological parents have a greater tendency to assume their child is like them and are more prone to misgauge their child's innate strengths and/or weaknesses. Biological parents will be misled if they expect a son or daughter, who may physically resemble a natural parent, to have that parent's intelligence, temperament, interests and skills. Parents should evaluate their biological children with discernment and objectivity, as if the children were adopted. Some children just seem to be more like us than others.

RAISING CHILDREN WHO ARE NOT LIKE US

Children born with personality characteristics such as aggressiveness, unresponsiveness to affection, learning differences, moodiness or sleeplessness will be particularly challenging for parents who come from families where these traits are foreign. There are no jokes about inheriting a grandmother's rigidity, an uncle's hyperactivity or an aunt's temper. Instead, the parents may become frustrated by the unfamiliarity of the child's response.

For example, some parents might bring their child for psychiatric evaluation because of bed wetting, possibly inherited from an unknown relative. Other parents, who themselves were bed-wetters, may wait patiently for their child to "grow out of it." Parents who are rigid, compulsive and serious may have great difficulty with a child who is disorganized, impulsive and volatile. In a different family this child's personality traits might be the norm.

Inherited physical, personality and intellectual characteristics of a child hold different importance to some families compared to others. Parents who have satisfying jobs that require no college degree might be more accepting of a child with a learning difference than parents who are college professors.

Intellectually gifted but physically uncoordinated children could be more appreciated in academic families than they would be by parents highly invested in sports. Children's inborn strengths and weaknesses will drive the direction of their personalities, but these inborn traits will be accepted, rewarded or criticized depending on the personalities and value systems of the parents. The parents' reaction to a child will greatly influence the child's self-image, self-esteem and self-confidence.

How parents manage their children will shape the children's behavior and how they adjust to society. A nine-year-old boy, Scott, since being a toddler, has been cautious, careful with his toys and responsive to his parents' commands. His eight-year-old sister, Samantha, is impulsive, careless with her possessions and must be told repeatedly before she obeys. The parents tell Scott and Samantha to clean up their room. Scott goes directly to his room and straightens the few items out of their regular place. Samantha initially ignores the request, then argues she is too busy and begins to cry, saying Scott messed up her room.

The parents recognize they will never change Samantha to be like Scott. However, Samantha still must clean her room; this means it will take effort by her parents to see that she does it. In the process, and through thousands of similar battles, Samantha will learn respect for authority, to control her impulsiveness and to appreciate the disadvantages of being disorganized and careless. Forcing Samantha to clean her room creates uproar for the family. In the short run, it would be easier to accept Samantha as "not being born to do housework."

Samantha, on the other hand, is always eager to play outside with her friends, enjoys sports and excels in athletics. Scott prefers to be inside, to watch TV and play video games. Scott tends to be overweight and the parents have to push Scott to exercise or be involved with peers. The parents realize Scott is different from Samantha, but this does not mean they should accept Scott as "being born to be a hermit."

Parents, depending on their own heritage and upbringing, may have more difficulty with a child like Samantha than like Scott, or vice-versa. This, of course, is no justification for avoiding confronting a child's behavior. In the final analysis, the parents make the difference whether children use inborn abilities to their best advantage. Parents, recognizing their children's frailties, must decide when to assist their children to avoid a problem or when to push them to overcome a weakness, permitting them to sink or swim. Such determinations come easily and naturally if you know your child. Parents are excellent judges of their children's ability if they spend time observing and interacting with them.

Family life can modify a child's inheritance, but the "genes in the jeans" exert a powerful force. There is a prayer used by Alcoholics Anonymous called the Serenity Prayer. It is, "Lord, give me the strength to change those things I should, the patience to accept those things I cannot change, and the wisdom to know the difference." It might be modified slightly to be useful for parents: "Lord give me time with my children so I understand them, give me the strength to change those things about them I should, the patience to accept those things I cannot change and the wisdom to know the difference." The first five years of a child's life are a crucial time to apply these principles.

CHAPTER THREE

THE IMPORTANT FIRST FIVE YEARS

TEACHING GOD'S COMMANDMENTS - A COMPUTER ANALOGY

Think of your infant child as the world's most sophisticated computer. Coming out of the box, it is turned on but can't do anything. You must install an operating system (the Ten Commandments) and provide other input that will make it largely autonomous within six years.

God has given us the instructions in the Bible and they are listed in the numerical order in which they need to be programmed. The main thing you need to do is make sure that the operating system is installed from Commandment One through Five, as the computer is designed to acquire artificial intelligence when the child is about six years old. From then on it will be increasingly programmed by forces outside of parental control.

God doesn't give parents tasks that are impossible. He expects you to be intentional about installing these first Five Commandments. God said this in Deuteronomy 6:7-9:

Impress them on your children. Talk about them when you sit at home and when you walk along the road, when you lie down and when you get up. Tie them as symbols on your hands and bind them on your foreheads. Write them on the doorframes of your houses and on your gates.

THE TEN COMMANDMENTS
Exodus 20:
And God spoke all these words:

1. "I am the LORD your God, who brought you out of Egypt, out of the land of slavery. "You shall have no other gods before me.

2. "You shall not make for yourself an image in the form of anything in heaven above or on the earth beneath or in the waters below. You shall not bow down to them or worship them; for I, the LORD your God, am a jealous God, punishing the children for the sin of the parents to the third and fourth generation of those who hate me, but showing love to a thousand generations of those who love me and keep my commandments.

3. "You shall not misuse the name of the LORD your God, for the LORD will not hold anyone guiltless who misuses his name.

4. "Remember the Sabbath day by keeping it holy. Six days you shall labor and do all your work, but the seventh day is a Sabbath to the LORD your God. On it you shall not do any work, neither you, nor your son or daughter, nor your male or female servant, nor your animals, nor any foreigner residing in your towns. For in six days the LORD made the heavens and the earth, the sea, and all that is in them, but he rested on the seventh day. Therefore the LORD blessed the Sabbath day and made it holy.

5. "Honor your father and your mother, so that you may live long in the land the LORD your God is giving you.

God is serious! Prototypes have different capabilities and God does not provide instructions that cover every step necessary for each unique model. The steps are clear. You are expected to figure it out how to get it done.

If your children have successfully integrated the first five Commandments, they will leave for kindergarten as well prepared as any child can be. Through honoring God, they will have learned to honor their parents, and through honoring their parents they will develop a lifelong respect for authority. It is extremely important that parents accomplish the task of having their children honor them by the time they start to school. It makes the school experience much more difficult if the teacher has to first teach the child to respect authority.

STAGES OF DEVELOPMENT

A child's personality emerges through a process that child psychiatrists know as "developmental lines." This concept describes how the child's personality passes through one stage, followed by another, usually in an orderly and predictable manner. For example, children crawl before they walk, and walk before they are able to run. An infant first coos, garbles, says words, then sentences, followed by the stepwise development of fluid speech.

Emotional growth proceeds in a similar fashion. Infants first bond to their mother, then learn they are separate and have their individual identities and then establish a degree of independence from their mother and begin to exert self-control. By approximately five years they proceed into the latency phase where energy is primarily devoted to making friends and learning in school. Following latency, adolescence begins with its own step-by-step developmental process.

Raising children is a time-limited joy and responsibility. Assuming children leave home at eighteen, they will have spent twenty-two percent of their lives under some influence of their parents. Conversely, seventy-eight percent of a parent's life will not involve child rearing. Parenting is relatively short. It behooves us to use this time advantageously.

THE PARENTING RACE

Parenting can be compared to running a race. In a race, maximum effort is needed at the beginning. If the runner gets off to a good start, the remainder of the race will go smoothly unless unforeseen complications arise. For parents, the start of the race begins with their child's first five years of life. At the child's start, parents need to devote their most concentrated effort. With a good first five years, the final thirteen years the child will have at home should go smoothly unless unexpected complications arise. Should these occur, successful parents make adjustments. They shift back into a sprint, increasing their time and effort with their children. With perseverance, prayer, and sometimes professional assistance, parents should be able to resume a more comfortable pace toward the finish.

Appreciating the importance of childhood and staying in the race is important. Children have a natural tendency to grow up healthy if they are protected and receive adequate guidance and nurture. Parents who have had a fairly normal childhood themselves (particularly if raised with religious influence), who love their child and devote time to their family, will automatically do most things right.

JESUS AS A CHILD

It might have been logical for Jesus to come to earth as a powerful adult who would rescue the Jews from their enemies. God must think having a childhood is important; why else would He have sent the Messiah, His Son Jesus Christ, to earth as an infant? The Bible suggests Jesus was raised like most other children. The people in His hometown, Nazareth, remember Him as being like everyone else. When Jesus returned as an adult to preach in Nazareth (Matthew 13:55), the people said, *"How is this possible? He is just a carpenter's son, and we know His mother and His brothers, James, Joseph, Simon, Judas, and His sisters."* It appears that even the Messiah was not raised like He was a Messiah.

PARENTING DURING THE FIRST FIVE YEARS

The first five years of a child's life are so crucial since they form the foundation of the personality. Think of the great change that occurs to the totally helpless baby from birth until 5 years of age when he/she will be heading to kindergarten or first grade. Parents have great responsibility and opportunity to positively impact children during the first five years. The only other time when the impact of parents is so critical is when children become teenagers, another time of accelerated physical and mental change. The big difference between the two stages is that the earlier period is so much easier and usually is a joy. Parents never again will be in such a position of power and control. Young children more easily give parents their love, respect and attention. Teenagers are more focused on becoming independent and free of parental control.

The first two years of a child's life are mostly impacted by the mother. Although this role can be filled by a mother substitute, usually there is no one who can project the love, protection and positive interaction with a child as the natural mother. If the infant is blessed to be born into an intact family, the father plays an important part. There is much more to it, but his major role during the first two years is mostly summarized by the cliche', "If Mamma isn't happy, no one is happy."

However, father needs to make the effort to be physically present as much as possible. Nurturing the infant is best when it is a joint operation. It is important for the father to be encouraging, assisting and expressing his appreciation for the mother's care-taking. The father should keep in mind that babies begin to absorb some sexual identity at an early age. The way he handles his son or insists on dressing him in blue jeans and athletic shoes may have some impact. The father being present may also influence the way the daughter relates to other males in the future. Personality characteristics such as his affection, empathy, self-confidence and competitiveness may be conveyed. What a daughter sees at home between her father and mother can influence what family model she chooses in the future.

By two years, managing the child becomes more obviously a two-person job. Parents need to encourage the child to become more independent, assure that he/she is toilet trained and has socialization skills that will happily head him/her off to kindergarten with his/her own little personality. It is important that by this time the child honors the mother and father, as this is the basis for respect for authority (to be discussed at length later in the book.).

Parents will make millions of decisions that will affect their children's lives. Fortunately a few hundred misguided parental actions usually do not counteract all the positive decisions parents make in their child's behalf. Parents who feel guilty that they have mishandled a particular conflict with their child will learn they will have many other opportunities to revisit the same issue.

Parents should keep in mind the goal of raising children is to assist them to become self-sufficient enough to safely leave home. Children are a gift on loan from God. Parents lose perspective when they raise children as their unique possessions.

The challenge is for parents to give children the considerable attention they need during childhood without causing them to feel entitled or to rob them of the opportunity to deal with adversity and develop strength of character. Parents' reaction to a child's particular behavior will need to vary, depending on the child's intellectual and emotional maturity. The younger the child, the more the parents will need to protect him or her from the outside world.

Successfully completing each developmental step opens unlimited possibilities for the next stage. Parents must adjust their methods as children mature.

In the first two years of children's lives there should be an emphasis on protecting and nurturing. Infants must feel secure and loved. Into the terrible twos and through age five, children need to learn self-control, to honor their father and mother, develop respect for authority, have a sense of sexual identity and to relate to other children in a give and take manner.

During grade school, children focus on academic learning, developing self-discipline, enjoying competition, playing by rules and establishing social relationships outside the family. In adolescence, parents must protect their teenagers whose judgment may be faulty, but not prevent them from becoming more independent.

When it is not too dangerous and when the consequences are not grave, children need to learn from experience. It takes involved and discerning parents to judge if a particular experience offers greater opportunity for growth or harm to their children.

Nothing during early childhood is more crucial for children than their parents' love and the love of God. There may be no time better for communicating this than when praying with them.

CHAPTER FOUR

PRAYER WITH YOUNG CHILDREN

Great men in the Bible, such as Abraham, Joseph, Moses, David, Jesus' disciples, Paul and Jesus Himself, were all fervent in prayer. In Paul's letter to Timothy (I Timothy 2:1), he listed in his *"instructions on worship"* that first there be prayer.

For a believer, prayer is an indispensable part of life. Many parents regularly pray for their children. These parents believe their faith and personal relationship with God through prayer gives them the wisdom and strength to guide and protect their children. I have observed the positive impact of parents' prayers on child rearing.

How do you want your children to remember you and what behaviors would you like for your children to emulate? In the process of prayer, we may be at our best as role models for our children. Thanking God for His protection and gifts, admitting our own shortcomings, seeking forgiveness and assistance to live according to God's will and asking help for others in need, projects a powerful, benevolent example for our children.

When you are praying, it is more likely you are sitting together at the dinner table or at a church picnic rather than in the neighborhood bar. The act of prayer automatically places families in more positive environments. When parents arrange opportunities for family prayer, they place their family in a wholesome, healthy environment.

Although parents more commonly pray in silence one-on-one with God, some praying should include the whole family. There are situations where family prayer seems to come naturally. These times include children saying their prayers with parents at bedtime, having a blessing with meals, praying in unison at church, and participating in a family devotional or Bible study.

PRAYER AT BEDTIME

If parents did not grow up in a family where prayer was routine, they may feel self-conscious when praying with their children. Praying, like most actions, gets more comfortable the more often we do it. It is easier if we start praying with our children when they are young. Tucking children into bed and helping them say their prayers is true "quality time" for parent and child. Bedtime prayer is also a way for parents to practice and become more comfortable praying publicly.

An innocent and trusting child provides a model for parents on how God wants us to approach Him. In Matthew 18:3-4, Jesus told His disciples, ***"Unless you turn to God from your sins and become as little children, you will never get into the Kingdom of Heaven. Therefore anyone who humbles himself as this little child, is the greatest in the Kingdom of Heaven."*** Bedtime prayer with a child may be a parent's first step in making prayer a regular part of family life. It can begin a lifelong habit of prayer for both parent and child.

PRAYER AT MEALTIME

Another natural, comfortable time for parents to pray is at dinner. Prayer at mealtime can be a springboard to improved communication in the family, and may identify specific needs of family members. Some families claim they are too busy to eat dinner together. Children need loving, wise, protective parental guidance. One place children receive such guidance is at dinner with their family, particularly when it begins with prayer.

The family dinner, a tradition for centuries, appears to be heading for oblivion. Today's high-tech, hectic lifestyle has made family dinner no longer routine. The older the children, the harder it is to have them regularly have dinner with the family. Work, school and athletic and social activities are given a higher priority. Getting the family together at mealtime requires determination, planning, and self-sacrifice. It is well worth the effort!

Most families find having dinner together warm and comfortable, as family members share experiences and plan upcoming activities. However, some families view eating dinner together as an unpleasant, if not dreaded, experience. Praying before meals can help defuse angry, bitter, mean-spirited communication.

During my group therapy with children, a snack is served. The children in the group often perceive it as being like a family. I am the "father," there is a female co- therapist, the "mother," and the children in the group see themselves as the "brothers" and "sisters." The group therapy allows more accurate diagnosis of the problems the children are having at home. Sadly, it may also give some children something they seldom received during childhood, a regular meal with their "parents."

Parents should realize if there is a problem having mealtime with their children, there is a problem. The solution is not to avoid mealtime. Family meals are an excellent barometer for judging how family members feel about each other. It is a good place to recognize and resolve minor conflicts before they become major problems. Add prayer, and parents will be stacking the deck in favor of their children's good mental health.

PRAYER AT CHURCH

If a parent wants to learn to pray, what easier way than to attend church? There, the congregation is coached in praying technique by listening to the minister, reading from prayer books, and being led by church leaders. When children accompany their parents to church, they will identify with their parents as the parents demonstrate their beliefs and values in prayer.

Is this not the image we want to project to our children? Where are we better? Church gives parents direction and support in establishing moral and ethical values for their children. It places both parent and child with others who have similar beliefs and demonstrates the benefit of having lives that are shaped by the Word of God. Regular attendance at church proves to children that their parents feel going to church and living godly lives is important.

I often hear parents say they want their children to have different (better) friends. Parents may conclude that the best place to look for these "better" friends is in a church. However, teenagers may be too afraid of rejection to try to make new friends in a church they did not grow up in.

Sometimes their fears may be justified. Some teenagers, even Christian ones, are not eager to add new friends to their group. If you want your children to have friends who have church values, get them to church early in their lives, and if the church in your neighborhood doesn't fit your personality, shop around. Choose a church whose leaders and members project a lifestyle you admire and believe to be Godly.

Taking children to church is the parents' responsibility. Few children prefer to attend church rather than sleep late or watch TV. Children are not capable of deciding whether organized religion and church attendance is useful to them.

Not attending church is one way teenagers assert their independence. Parents may give in to their resistance to go to church, rationalizing this is a normal developmental step for the teenager. They are just "growing up." True, it is important teenagers begin to make their own decisions and become more independent from their parents. However, there are thousands of opportunities for them to become independent without allowing them to withdraw from the positive influence of regular church attendance. Parents can loosen ties to their children in many ways. Church attendance is one place where parents should stand their ground!

As children go through adolescence, their parents may seem old fashioned and oppressive, but other adults may seem "cool" and can become role models and/or mentors. Although not all people in church are good, church is one of the best places I know to find other adults who can be a positive influence for your children. Church can be a protective, stabilizing, guiding support system for parents and children. When a parent is learning to pray, a good place to start might be, "Please God, keep my child under the protection and influence of a church."

THE FAMILY DEVOTIONAL

Another occasion for family prayer is a family devotional. Prepared lessons designed for regular, family devotions are available through most churches. These family discussion times may focus on values, behaviors, family relationships, and will begin and/or end with prayer. For parents who seldom pray in the home, who infrequently attend church and whose friends are not religious, having a family devotional may seem too much to ask.

Some parents are more comfortable using family "meetings" to improve communication, work out family conflicts and plan family activities. From my point of view, either the family meeting or the family devotional could be very useful. Although both can accomplish the same psychological purpose, the devotional is one more way for the parents to demonstrate to their children that God and His teachings are important.

Commonly, when a psychiatrist evaluates an emotionally disturbed child, a problem in family communication and family interaction is discovered. Family therapy may be recommended. Having a psychiatrist help a family communicate and work out family conflicts in family therapy can feel more awkward and uncomfortable than a family devotional, and certainly is more expensive.

Some parents first turn to prayer when faced with a family crisis. Although prayer may calm a vicious divorce or provide direction for a troubled child, these painful life situations might never have occurred if prayer had always been a part of the family's life.

The result of parents' prayer is seldom immediate. Its effect may not be fully appreciated until the children are almost grown. Putting children to bed with prayer, having children together for dinner with a blessing, praying with children during regular church attendance, and praying at a weekly family devotional, quietly but steadily, shapes children and parents into what God wants them to become. Parents praying with their children is an important way for them to identify themselves as messengers of God's love.

CHAPTER FIVE

PARENTS: MESSENGERS FOR GOD'S LOVE

The most damaging of all parents are those who give their children no love. Psychiatrists are quick to recognize the importance of love for a child. Scientific writings, such as those of Bowlby (Note 1), Harlow (Note 2) and Spitz (Note 3) attest to the danger of unavailable, insufficient or inadequate parental love. Without love and attention, an infant may suffer mental retardation or die. Through the loving, protective relationship of parents, a child learns basic trust and develops self-esteem. Sigmund Freud's equivalent of love, libido, is said to be the fundamental drive that shapes all personal relationships.

The message of God's love pervades the Bible. The Old Testament repeatedly depicts God's love as He commands, guides, reprimands, and forgives His chosen people. The New Testament stresses the love of God, shown by the sacrifice of His Son for our sins. John 3:16 clearly explains this love, ***"for God so loved the world that He gave His only Son that whosoever believes in Him shall not perish but shall have everlasting life."*** Paul said in I Corinthians 13:13, ***"There are three things that remain - faith, hope, and love - and the greatest of these is love."***

Parents have a responsibility to teach their children of God's love (Deuteronomy 6:7, Psalms 22:30). However, very young children have difficulty grasping the concept of God. They look to parents for love and protection. Parents, not God, hold and soothe them. Parents, not God, hug and kiss them. Parents, not God, tell them they are loved. Parents, not God, look under the bed and in the closet to assure them when they are frightened. Parents, not God, clothe and feed them. Young children experience God's love through their parents.

Being God's messenger to their children requires that parents understand the message. If parents don't know what God's love is like, they will either convey it inaccurately or make up their own personalized version. In John 15:12, Jesus commanded we love one another as He loves us. The Bible is the place to learn how God loves us.

Some parents overvalue the impact of telling their children they love them, minimizing that God's love also includes protecting, teaching, disciplining and punishing. For example, Moses and David, both greatly loved by God, were punished for their transgressions.(Numbers 20:7-12). 2 Samuel 12:13-18).

UNCONDITIONAL LOVE

Although the Old Testament repeatedly demonstrates God's love and forgiveness and the New Testament says God's love is not earned but given, neither called God's love "unconditional." In Luke 15:11-31, the story of the prodigal son, Jesus describes a parent who welcomes the return of his wayward son. Although sometimes quoted as an example of God's unconditional love, to me it seems a better example of God's capacity to forgive. The father's reception of his prodigal son may not have been as warm if the son had not asked his father's forgiveness and renounced his former lifestyle.

I discussed this concept of unconditional love with several ministers and friends. One minister said she felt "unrelenting" was more accurate than "unconditional" in describing God's love. From my clinical experience, overemphasis of unconditional love can be unhealthy for children.

Although it is destructive for children to experience chronic failure and loss of hope, it is also damaging to love their frailties away by overprotecting them from adversity. Some children develop outstanding study habits as they struggle to compensate for a learning disorder. On the other hand, some students give up immediately if an academic task requires effort, because they have grown accustomed to being allowed to bypass difficult work.

In Romans 5:3-4, Paul says we should rejoice in our trials and problems as they are good for us and build strength of character. This does not mean parents should not help their children. Parents can assist and encourage children to attempt tasks, which will blossom into satisfying accomplishments. Parents, by supporting and praising their children's positive behavior, can promote self-esteem based on reality and competence.

SELF-ESTEEM

Parents may use unconditional love as a method for building their child's self-esteem. The quest for self-esteem can cause parents to prime their children's social life by providing increasingly expensive toys, birthday parties or trips that will attract friends and make the children popular. These children may avoid learning the give and take of interpersonal relationships, relying on their parents to provide friends. When this contrived popularity can no longer be sustained, the children are hurt. Such practices rob the children of opportunities to develop other real strengths they possess.

Parents can avoid such pitfalls by measuring their children by Heavenly standards rather than worldly standards. Worldly criteria for measuring children's successes are fickle. What is "in" today can become "uncool" tomorrow. What a frustrating and unrewarding task for a child to chase such changing, and often unrealistic, ideals. What a weight would be taken off their shoulders if children believed God, not popular opinion, was their judge.

It is not always easy to live a life that is pleasing to God, but we all come with the tools to accomplish it. We don't have to be pretty, smart, strong, agile, clever or rich. Wouldn't it make a difference if our children realized this? Wouldn't it be a relief? Wouldn't they feel more self-confident? Couldn't this be their basis for self-esteem? It is so much more reasonable and fulfilling to teach our children the clear and lasting criteria as described in the Bible for pleasing God.

"Self-esteem" is our culture's buzzword. Self-esteem is important for a child. However, it should be an esteem steeped in the child, developing true competence, not a phony sense of "I am a wonderful person because I am." In Romans 12:3, Paul says, *"As God's messenger I give each of you God's warning: be honest in your estimate of yourself."*

There is no place in the Bible where parents are told to try to develop self-esteem in their children. If there is a reference to self-esteem in the Bible, it is in the context of being secure and unafraid because we are created in the image of God (Genesis 1:27). In Matthew 10:29, Jesus tells us if He watches over the sparrows in the sky, then He certainly will care for us. This faith that children are of unique value because of the love of God is very different from the self-esteem manufactured by many in today's culture. It is the emphasis on the self and the neglect of the importance of the love of God that can corrupt the self-esteem principle.

GOD'S LOVE

It seems a shame that parents seldom mention to their children how special it is that God loves the children. Children feel protected, secure and comforted when they are told God loves them. Children delight in singing, "Yes, Jesus loves me, the Bible tells me so." Teaching children they are loved by God also helps parents. It is not good for parents to become their children's "god." Even if parents have immense affection and dedication to child rearing, parents are not always loving. Accepting God's love for children relieves parents of the impossible task of being perfect. When parents assume responsibility for providing all of a child's love, it leaves the child uniquely vulnerable to loss. Parents may be separated from their children by divorce, illness or death. What a comfort for children and parents to know that whatever happens, God will always be there for them. God's love is omnipresent.

Children who grow up knowing God loves them should be secure, confident and unafraid. Parents, God's messengers, must deliver this hopeful lesson. When parents are carrying the message of God's love, they are spending quality time with their children.

CHAPTER SIX

WHAT IS "QUALITY TIME?"

Most time parents spend with children can be considered quality time. It includes times of fun, difficultly and dullness. Parents have a tendency to see quality time as only when parent and child share a special experience that leaves parents with a warm feeling of unique camaraderie or friendship. Examples I have heard include watching a son land a big bass, a mother helping her daughter into her first party dress or having a family picnic or vacation. Those are memorable times, but stockpiling these elusive quality times is not the crux of being a loving and effective parent. Instead, they are the frosting on the cake, the strokes we need to encourage us to continue the work of parenting when we might otherwise tire.

Quality time is when parents are implementing the message of God's love described in the previous chapters. Jesus Christ's relationship with His disciples, who He referred to as "children," is an excellent model for what quality time can be. Jesus spent time with, and was an example for, His children. Jesus protected His disciples, but also prepared them to go out on their own. Jesus sacrificed for His children and taught them how to receive the gift of eternal life.

SPEND TIME WITH YOUR CHILDREN

Once Jesus began His ministry, He lived night and day with His disciples. Jesus spent considerable time with His "children." At today's hectic pace, often with both parents working, parents time with their children may be limited. Parents frequently ask how they can be more effective with their child-time, how they can make it quality time? In responding to their question, I must be careful not to support a notion that the total time spent with their children is less important than the desired quality time. No matter how you fine-tune parenting, it requires time and requires large amounts of it. Sometimes when parents become more efficient with their child time, they use the time saved for other self-fulfilling activities.

When my own children were young and I was working hard to build a child psychiatric practice, I was much less available to them than I am today. Sometimes, when listening attentively, free of interruptions and distractions, to one of my child patients, I realized sadly what a unique experience this is for a child. Can you imagine the impact of both parents devoting one hour a week exclusively to listen to, understand, and enjoy each of their children? Think what it would do for the child, and the parent-child relationship, if this was done weekly for the eighteen or nineteen years the child lived at home. Listening to children with care and letting them know their thoughts and feelings are of concern to you, can be a vital step in maintaining a life-long mutual relationship of respect and love.

Children whose parents are available to them are more secure, confident and happy. Having a parent at home provides more control over how a young child's life is structured. Children's personality and character should develop more steadily and smoothly when there is routine and consistency in their lives. Regular meals, nap time, bath time, prayer time and bedtime are ways to provide structure for children. Putting routine into children's lives allows them to invest their energies in learning and relating to others, instead of trying to anticipate and adjust to a frantic and shifting family environment.

I remember evaluating Tommy, a five-year-old boy who had been expelled from two preschools because he was hyperactive and had cursed and hit his teachers. He was also out of control at home, refusing to go to his bedroom to sleep and running away when his parents corrected him. At mealtime, Tommy would not eat anything but pizza and hotdogs and would disrupt the meal with demanding, belligerent behavior. The parents brought him for psychiatric evaluation, thinking he might have attention deficit disorder (ADD).

Tommy was observed to be an energetic, athletic five-year-old with no obvious signs of an emotional problem. Ritalin was prescribed; largely to rule out the possibility his diagnosis was attention deficit disorder. As the medicine produced only slight improvement, I did not recommend that it be continued. Shortly after Tommy saw me, he left for Maine to stay with his maternal grandparents for one month.

The following is a letter the grandparents wrote to Tommy's parents that they copied to me. The names of the parents (Nicole and Robert) and the grandparents (Alice and Frank) have been changed.

Nicole and Robert:
We would like to put into writing some of our thoughts after being involved with Tommy since the middle of June and most especially the past three weeks. Although we certainly are not experts in child behavior, or do we claim to be perfect parents, the following will be our observations and suggestions regarding Tommy and what will work for him toward his future development.

The most significant thing we see is that he requires structure in his life. By that we mean he responds well to having scheduled mealtimes, bedtimes, specific types of playtime, quiet time upon approaching bedtime, etc. In doing this we have found that he will sleep in his own bed willingly. He goes to sleep peacefully after a bedtime story (with no television going). His excuses for not doing this in the beginning were numerous and varied. We ignored them and proceeded with our program. At mealtime, he now sits at the table with adults using his utensils and napkin, which is required, and eats what is put in front of him. This includes vegetables, fruit of all kinds, different meats and soup. Milk is the mealtime drink. The only time he gets dessert is when he finishes his entire meal, and this is his decision.

We have tried and feel it works to reinforce consistent behavior. This means that we do, and he does, the same things the same way every time. Manners are part of this consistent behavior as well as treating other people the way you want to be treated in return. To accomplish this we sometimes had to be firm with Tommy. If you say something is to be a certain way, you must carry through with it - because if you give him an inch, he'll take a mile every time.

We have enjoyed having Tommy with us. For the most part; he's been a very happy and cooperative little guy - seemingly well adjusted to his three-week visit with us. He's been very social, and has fit into every situation that we've exposed him to.

I hope this will help you - and I'm going to send a copy of this to Dr. Myers - hoping that all of this input will only help Tommy to fit into the big world that is waiting for him as he grows and matures.
Love,
    Alice and Frank

When Tommy came in to see me after his visit with his grandparents, he was more relaxed and calmer than when I had seen him before. His parents said Tommy was now easier to control, and he was sleeping in his own bed. All of us agreed Tommy did not have ADD and that Ritalin was not the answer for his problems.

Nicole and Robert said they had difficulty establishing family routine because their jobs were demanding and required long and inconsistent work hours. Both parents acknowledged they let most of Tommy's behavior go unchallenged, because it was easier to let him have his way than to spend so much time arguing with him. The focus of the therapy shifted to helping the parents establish more structure, routine and consistency in their home.

PARENTS MUST SACRIFICE

Being a parent does not require the magnitude of sacrifice Jesus made for His children, but, done properly, it will require considerable sacrifice. Parents will find they can no longer be as pleasure-seeking as many of their single friends. Mothers who choose to have children should accept that it might limit what they might have accomplished in a career. Likewise, a career may limit what can be accomplished as a mother. Both can easily require a full time commitment. Being a mother is a career for millions of women, but there is what I consider a hopeful trend of mothers returning to the home.

Of course, many modern couples share parenting responsibility in ways that are far removed from the traditional hunter and gatherer stereotypes of the past. In some families the female is the primary wage earner, while the male remains at home to care for the children. Today, there are varying blends of the traditional mother and father roles. The Bible does not specify that only the mother should meet the emotional needs of the children. Jesus' comments and interactions with children seemed characteristic of the way a mother might relate. He was eager to have children around him and described children as models for learning how to approach God. He also related to his disciples, whom he called "children," with a mothering quality.

One of the advantages of the father taking on mothering responsibility is that it involves him more actively in the parenting process. It also makes him appreciate the labor and joys of motherhood. Such fathers are more supportive and helpful to their wives. Done wisely, blending parental responsibility gives both parents greater satisfaction and support. This method provides a model for the children to emulate as they see their parents' helpfulness, respect, and love for one another.

Unfortunately, when some parents blend parental responsibility, no one chooses to be the mother. Someone must take this role. True parental role reversals must be considered experimental. The jury is still out on what type of adults will grow from such arrangements. There are thousands of years of experience with a mother being a woman. I tend to go with that - others might argue that the state of the world today suggests it is time for a change.

Well-intentioned couples plan carefully how they can provide good care for a child without compromising either of their careers. If husband and wife decide they must skimp on their time with children, perhaps they should reconsider whether they should have children. There are opportunities other than parenthood for meeting an adult's maternal and paternal needs. Some include Big Brothers, volunteer work in child social agencies, coaching children's sports and caring for a niece or nephew. Popular slogans such as "I want it all," "I want to be my own person," "Just do it!" and "Go for it!" have a hollow ring when they are superimposed on shaping a child's life.

It certainly is possible to have a career and be a successful mother. My adult children seem to have managed it. However, skillful orchestration is necessary, and ideally there will be few unplanned crises such as illness, pregnancy, marital discord or job transfers. There must be flexible working hours which will allow the mother to first respond to her children when there is a special and immediate need. It will increase chances of success if there is an understanding, supportive spouse who also has a job that lets him take time off to help. Remarkable judgment and good luck will be needed to choose child-care centers, baby-sitters, drivers, tutors and other helpers who will be able to adequately assist a parent.

It would be interesting to compare the money made by both parents, working during the first five years of a child's life, with the extra cost of caring for and treating an insecure and unhappy child. Maladjusted children require special services that can quickly eat away earlier savings. Consider the costs of psychological or educational testing, tutors, special schools, in addition to child, family and/or parental counseling.

Should a child's difficulties progress to alcohol or drug abuse, depression, antisocial behavior or other forms of mental illness, costs can become astronomical. Having a parent at home is a big advantage to a child. A decision for both parents to work in order to provide more material possessions for their children, or to provide their children more stimulating life experiences, may be shortsighted and can be a mistake financially.

The first five years of a child's life are when the foundation, walls and roof of children's personalities are being constructed; it is important their carpenters (loving parents) are working on the job. Subcontracting child rearing can lead to a shoddy result.

BE AN EXAMPLE

Jesus was an example for His disciples. Similarly, children identify with their parents. A child is like a recording camcorder or a sponge soaking up the personality of his parents. Proverbs 20:7 says, *"It is a wonderful heritage to have an honest father."* When children are in the presence of their parents, they incorporate their parents' attitudes, values, beliefs and behaviors. Neither parents nor children fully appreciate that children's camcorders usually remain on. Sometimes the playback of the parents' personalities does not demonstrate itself for years.

Discovering we have developed mannerisms, thought patterns and habits that belonged to our parents should be a clear signal, or warning, that our children absorb our own character. Children's camcorders will pick up important attitudes and beliefs of the parents, as well as minute, seemingly insignificant information. For example, I saw one young adult who had elaborately tattooed his body, justifying his action because one parent has a small, inconspicuous tattoo. Incidentally, it was a surprise to read in the Bible (*Leviticus 19:28*) that God forbid tattooing.

When I was jogging in the morning, I would regularly dodge parents who ignore stop signs as they drive their children to school. Like all other children, those children have their "camcorders" running. The parents may find that when these children begin driving, they disregard the parents' instructions to "stop for stop signs." Who would imagine that a mother running a stop sign today could endanger her teenage children ten years later?

Family interests may be passed down by identification. For example, a man is an avid golfer. His grandfather and his father also played golf. Is it surprising his son is on the high school golf team? None of these men ever told their sons to play golf. They just identified with their fathers.

My wife was raised in a family where many activities revolved around their church and the friends she made there. As an adult she continued to attend church regularly and was a good Christian role model for her children. Her children, my stepchildren, continue this religious heritage. Their children and their children's children will live their lives by Christian principles. What a wonderful gift to pass on to children!

Jesus was perfect as an example for His disciples. What He taught was entirely consistent with the way He thought, felt and lived. As human parents, we can not be perfect, but the behavior Jesus teaches for adults in the Bible are the same we want for our children. If one is obedient to the Word of God, and is respectful, loving, kind, caring, industrious and honest, his or her child will more likely develop these qualities.

Unfortunately, children will identify with our bad example. The most certain indicator I have found for children who will abuse drugs is that their parents use them. How can it be bad if the people they love, trust and respect the most (their parents) do it? Even when parents use marijuana "recreationally," it can have disastrous consequences for their children.

Parents, who seem to have successful lives but continue to use drugs, typically began their drug use late in childhood or after they were adults, already having accomplished many developmental tasks. For example, they have become comfortable with their sexual identity, dated, made friendships not based largely on mutual drug use, probably completed high school and made progress in pursuing a college education and/or gainful employment. However, their children may not be so fortunate. The children of these parents may begin using drugs before such tasks are accomplished.

If marijuana is illegal in the state the family lives in, the parents' who smoke it will generally associate with other people who have a compromised, personalized view of what is right and wrong. Parents will avoid contact with people who would be critical of their drug use, therefore depriving the children of wholesome life experiences and positive influences that could help guide and direct them. For example, drug-using parents are less likely to take their children to church. Parents must never delude themselves into thinking they can hide their pot smoking from their children. Their camcorders see the truth.

Sometimes we have parts of our personality that are hidden, even to ourselves. Parents, without realizing it, can reinforce a child's behavior that consciously they are trying to extinguish. For example, a father may punish his son for spending so much of his time "chasing after girls," yet the father may secretly enjoy hearing of his son's sexual exploits. It is no wonder the father is ineffective in controlling his son's behavior. The father's true thoughts and feelings influenced his son more than his words. "Do as I say and not as I do," has little place in child rearing. Children identify with what we do and who we really are.

PROTECT, BUT ALSO PREPARE

When children are young, parents have the best opportunity to modify children's behaviors and character traits. As trees which grow crooked must be set straight while young, so children need attention early in life if they are to change. As early as one, two, or three years of age, parents can observe behaviors that signal future difficulties for their child. By three years of age, some children can be described as demanding, selfish, inflexible, angry, cruel, disrespectful, insatiable, unappreciative, dishonest, a loner, unhappy, impulsive, risk taking, stubborn, fearful, and countless other negative, as well as positive, attributes.

True, some of these characteristics represent a "stage" children are passing through. The problem with this assumption is some parents don't realize children's successful passages through their "stage" are largely determined by how parents deal with the behavior. Without caring, wise, determined parents to confront and shape children, they could stay in the "terrible twos" the rest of their lives.

Parents should see problem behaviors as an opportunity to correct unhealthy personality traits.

Children have a natural tendency to want immediate pleasure and will resist when parents thwart their wishes and, thus, conflict will occur. Dealing with conflict is an important aspect of quality time. During early childhood, parents have power, influence and control that will not exist in the future. The earlier parents confront and resolve difficulties with their children the better.

Families provide a base from which children can safely test new skills. When there is inordinate risk for children, parents must limit and buffer the children from danger. By cautiously allowing more independence and separation from the family, parents prepare children to go out on their own and make it possible for them to learn from others. Making the correct decision when to protect a child and when to let go is the essence of parenting. It requires maturity, wisdom, and hopefully divine guidance.

Even if a parent understands the risks and advantages to a child, there are decisions that involve complex probabilities. Do you let your children walk to school by themselves? It will depend on the distance to the school, the traffic, the type of neighborhood, the weather, your child's intelligence, maturity, attention span, mood, the personalities of the children they will walk with, whether they are rushed to get to school that day and numerous other factors. Many child-rearing decisions involve risk. What are the odds? Do you let your child play football? Go to camp? Get a hardship license? Spend the night with a friend? See an R-rated movie? Car date? Drink alcohol at home? Smoke cigarettes? Try to control who are their friends? Set a strict curfew?

Repeated exposure to the same risk increases the probability of something bad happening. For example, if you let your children stay out until 2:00 a.m. on one night, there may be only one chance in fifty that they will get into trouble. If you let them stay out for fifty nights, statistically there is one hundred percent chance that they will get into trouble on one of those nights. This may be highly significant because, for teenagers today, getting into trouble is not the harmless prank of years past. Today getting into trouble can mean drug abuse, AIDS, or drive-by shooting.

Making and implementing crucial parenting decisions requires parents to have spent enough time with their children to know their strengths and vulnerabilities. They must also know and assess their children's friends, as friends will strongly influence a children's behavior. It is helpful to have met their friends' parents so a united front can be presented with the other parents if a particular activity or behavior of the children must be curtailed. Knowing the parents may also give you an indication of the value system of their children. Parents must know where their children are, what they are doing and what degree of risk the activities present. The process of obtaining this information and making the most correct decision for your child is also quality time. Parents' commitment only to fun times with their children is no substitute for the loving, but often unappreciated effort parents put into making these decisions.

Quality time with parents should produce children who both love and respect their parents. However, sometimes it seems like children don't respond to parents like they used to.

CHAPTER SEVEN

CHILDREN ARE NOT LIKE THEY USED TO BE

Growing up in Texas in the 1950s, there were times when conflict between two teenage boys became so intense that we would "fight it out." However, even if we felt rage toward an adversary, there were limits on how our anger would be expressed. We called it "fighting fair." Only the two boys with the disagreement would fight. For two or three to jump on one was seen as cowardly. No weapons were used. For one boy to attack another with a club would have been unthinkable. There would be no scratching or biting. Most of us had never heard of karate, and kicking was not allowed. Once your adversary was down, the fight was over. Never, never, would someone kick his opponent when he was on the ground.

Today's youth would laugh at our rules for a fair fight. Not long ago I read of two teenagers from prestigious Dallas high schools meeting to fight over a girl. One had a friend with him, the other brought several. Ten to fifteen boys attacked two, eventually clubbing and kicking them to the ground, where one of the teenagers then tried to gouge out his rival's eyes. Children are very different than they were in the 50s.

In my practice of child and adolescent psychiatry, I have evaluated and treated children for five decades. The pattern is clear. American children are becoming insensitive to the rules that allow people to live safely and in harmony with one another. They are more prone to violence. Law officers will tell you that their most dangerous task is trying to arrest an armed teenager. Our children are less civilized. Some of them have become savages.

MADE IN GOD'S IMAGE?

The Bible says God made man in his own image. If we are, it doesn't seem like we have stayed that way. Thirty- five hundred years ago, God wrote a few clear, simple, irrefutable instructions telling human beings how to live in a peaceful, civilized manner. He wrote these Ten Commandments on two stone tablets and gave these to Moses on Mt. Sinai:

THE TEN COMMANDMENTS
Exodus 20:

And God spoke all these words:

1. "I am the LORD your God, who brought you out of Egypt, out of the land of slavery. "You shall have no other gods before me.

2. "You shall not make for yourself an image in the form of anything in heaven above or on the earth beneath or in the waters below. You shall not bow down to them or worship them; for I, the LORD your God, am a jealous God, punishing the children for the sin of the parents to the third and fourth generation of those who hate me, but showing love to a thousand generations of those who love me and keep my commandments.

3. "You shall not misuse the name of the LORD your God, for the LORD will not hold anyone guiltless who misuses his name.

4. "Remember the Sabbath day by keeping it holy. Six days you shall labor and do all your work, but the seventh day is a Sabbath to the LORD your God. On it you shall not do any work, neither you, nor your son or daughter, nor your male or female servant, nor your animals, nor any foreigner residing in your towns. For in six days the LORD made the heavens and the earth, the sea, and all that is in them, but he rested on the seventh day. Therefore the LORD blessed the Sabbath day and made it holy.

5. "Honor your father and your mother, so that you may live long in the land the LORD your God is giving you.
6. "You shall not murder.
7. "You shall not commit adultery.
8. "You shall not steal.
9 "You shall not give false testimony against your neighbor.
10. "You shall not covet your neighbor's house. You shall not covet your neighbor's wife, or his male or female servant, his ox or donkey, or anything that belongs to your neighbor."

Ironically, in light of today's headlines, commandment number six (Exodus 20: 13), *"You shall not murder"* may be the only commandment that the majority of Americans agree is relevant. The Bible's prohibitions against adultery, stealing, lying and coveting are considered outdated by many. Many Americans accept adultery as a way of life. Although we recognize robbery and theft as wrong, white- collar crime has become commonplace. Even under oath, lying is felt to be justified, if there seems to be a "good reason" for not telling the truth. Coveting and envy are seldom even remembered as being prohibited.

The Bible calls these ten rules "Commandments" for a reason. The stone tablets brought down by Moses did not record God's "Ten Suggestions." "Do not murder" is sound advice. That it comes from the Bible should not prejudice even an atheist against its merit. To ignore the 4000 years of life experience found in the Bible, because it is spiritual, would be foolish.

Our legal system is based on these Biblical principles. Teaching them is fundamental to guiding a child into adulthood. Whether one accepts Freud's notion that children are born with animal-like instincts or the Bible's assertion that children are innately sinful, the remedy is the same. Both the

Bible and modern psychiatry and psychology conclude that children require training. If parents do not actively guide and instruct their children, the children's immoral or animal-like behaviors will prevail.

REALITY OR FANTASY?

Psychiatrists call the ability to distinguish what is real compared to what is fantasy or illusion "reality-testing." It is the most obvious deficit of the severely mentally ill. Having hallucinations (seeing or hearing what is not there) and delusions (inaccurate and false beliefs, often of a paranoid nature) are the hallmark of psychotic illness. Children who have hallucinations and/or delusions may be diagnosed as schizophrenic or bipolar.

Most scientists believe that children with such disorders are born with abnormalities of their brain chemistry. It is as if the disturbed child is living in a dream or nightmare state. This type of disturbed reality testing is usually easily identified; as such children appear different or peculiar.

Children without obvious mental illness can also develop a distorted sense of what is real. The excessive and confusing stimuli of today's world make it difficult for even a normal child to distinguish the difference between reality, fantasy, and illusion.

In the past, objects that were real could be recognized by their appearance, feel or smell. Technology is blurring such traditional criteria. Through digital imaging, photographs and vocal recording can be altered and superimposed so that one can no longer trust the truth of what is seen or heard.

Through robotics and special effects, theme parks so closely resemble the real thing that the visitors feel like they are experiencing actual adventure and danger. Virtual reality allows the participant to be in a game and experience first hand many of the fears and thrills of combatants.

Computer games glamorize aggression and violence. However, the human suffering caused by killing is not depicted. Feelings such as a "sense of loss" or "grief" are not conveyed. The life the child experiences on the computer has no protective parental influence. Children play computer games free from reality and moral teachings. Escaping into violent computer fantasy may not significantly impact an adult. However, children, particularly those who spend four to six hours each day on the computer, may lose some grasp on reality.

Child and teenage chat rooms are not a satisfactory alternative to being entertained by computer games. Although chat rooms provide an opportunity for children to practice social skills, teenagers can give unhealthy advice to one another. Secretly arranged meetings with persons only known through the Internet can present real danger. Increasingly, parents seek psychiatric treatment for their teens because they have been traumatized by such incidents.

IS THERE AN ANTIDOTE?

Christians suspect that the decadent, sinful nature of our current culture is caused by it not being guided by the values God describes in the Bible. The self-indulgent behavior of media stars is glamorized and emulated. Worldliness has become an idol for many. Where are parents to turn if they are to shield and help their child cope in a confused and sinful world? Without clear guidance, parents are adrift.

Once, I asked a five-year-old child patient what he would like to be when he grows up? It surprised me when he answered, "I want to grow up to be a good person." Children like this little boy offer hope for an antidote to today's troubled times. His parents are God-fearing, religious people who have raised their child in a home directed by God's Word as found in the Bible. They comfortably follow God's instructions, finding the way smooth and uncomplicated. Such parents are no longer the rule. Many of today's parents have grown up without appreciating that God's law has relevance. As our nation becomes increasingly affluent and technologically advanced, we are becoming more self-indulgent, undisciplined, intolerant, immoral and violent. The Ten Commandments are God's blueprint of how to form a civilized society from an unruly, irreverent, cruel people. They provide a foundation that prevents chaos, bringing the order necessary for safe human relationships. The antidote for our post-Christian culture is a God-centered home. We must again teach and heed God's law. There are savages to be civilized today. Some are our children! Teaching God's laws can give them a good and long life.

CHAPTER EIGHT

GIVING YOUR CHILD A GOOD AND LONG LIFE

The Ten Commandments give clear instruction on how we are to relate to God and to one another. Of these commandments, Commandment V: ***"Honor your father and mother"*** is unique. It tells us "What to do," rather than "what not to do" in our human relationships. It is the only commandment giving directions specifically for family living. It is the only commandment that comes with a promise from God. Exodus 20:12 says if we honor our father and mother, we will have a good and long life.

Children who grow up failing to honor their parents violate a direct commandment of God. It has been my observation that such children will be undisciplined and have poor respect for authority. They are often troubled, unhappy and less likely to live the good and long life God promises.

From my psychiatric perspective, next to loving your child, assuring that your child honors his/her father and mother is the most crucial task a parent can accomplish to protect their child from a troubled life. Honoring their father and mother is the platform from which parents' discipline of their children should begin. Discipline of children is weakened or ineffective if children have no respect for their parents.

Failure of children to honor their father or mother can begin as early as the first year of life. During the first year, children will begin their passage through the stage of absolute dependency and become more separate from their parents. In a natural and gradual fashion, parents teach their children that they are not in command of the world.

WHO IS IN CHARGE?

Parents who are not aware of Biblical direction may have no clear standard for setting children's values and character. Their interactions with their children are largely driven by what makes the children happy. This can also give children unhealthy power over their parents. Parents may perpetuate children's sense of power unknowingly.

For example, today's parents spend a significant amount of time with their children in a car. Car time can be an excellent opportunity for parents and children to communicate. Sometimes parents may be so preoccupied with their own thoughts or cell phone they ignore what is going on with their children. More often it is the children choosing to ignore the parents. The children arrive at my office listening to music with headphones, assuring they did not have to talk to their mother, usually the driver. Routinely permitting such behavior confirms to children that what parents have to say is unimportant. Requiring that a child pay attention and engage the parent in conversation creates more respect for the parent and also shows the child that the parent values his/her ideas and opinions.

Parents can be so self-sacrificing it causes the children to have an unrealistic approach to life. Parents who themselves endured hardship and/or neglect as children may be too intent on seeing that their child does not "go through what they went through." Parents who spend little time with their children may try to make it up to them by over-indulging them.

Children who are overindulged can feel so special and privileged that they become condescending and inconsiderate with other children and adults. Even if parents are comfortable jumping to the demands of their own children, other adults will be critical of the children's attitude and behavior. These children irritate and anger others, and they will find the outside world unfriendly and rejecting. The child's response to this rejection can vary from changing his or her attitude and becoming sensitive to authority, to living a life of alienation and conflict.

If children act like tyrants at home, it is likely they will be disrespectful to adults when they are away. Most children do not have the discernment or self-control to act one way with family and another way when away from home.

Parents need not provide the best for the child instead of themselves. What incentive do children have to work to achieve the things their parents have, when they grow up being given many privileges of adulthood? It is not selfish for the parent to take the choice portion, own a better bicycle or automobile than their child, or go to Europe when their child hasn't been. It is understandable why some children grow up feeling they, not their parents, should be honored.

ESTABLISHING AUTHORITY

What can a parent do to gain honor and respect? The first step in developing a Biblically directed relationship with your child is to accept *"honor your father and mother"* as a crucial goal for your child. It is a natural, healthy and Godly phenomenon. Being honored carries a responsibility some parents want to avoid. It may be a signal to these parents they are really grown up. It does not allow them to be the just the child's playmate, as it emphasizes their parental role. Having a child may force a parent to mature. 1 Corinthians 13:11 says, *"When I was a child I thought and spoke and reasoned as a child does. But when I became a man my thoughts grew far beyond those of my childhood, and now I have put away the childish things."* Parents may need to change some of their own attitudes and behaviors. For example, it may be more difficult to teach your child respect for authority if you yourself are weak in this area. Parents can help each other with this issue. If a child is disrespectful to his/her mother, the father should quickly intervene, and vice versa. Parents, by the way they relate to each other, should demonstrate an attitude of honor and respect. If parents speak rudely to each other, the child may do the same.

Parents will not need to look to find ways they can demonstrate their authority to their child. A child's natural egocentric attitude will clash with the needs of other family members and some conflict is inevitable. To children's dismay, they realize parents decide when children wake up, when and what they eat, when they bathe and what time they go to bed. Parents who can implement such routines assure that their child gets adequate sleep, exercise, nutrition, and has good personal hygiene. Settling these issues early in a child's life will greatly decrease whining, crying, temper tantrums, colds, finicky eating, fatigue, tardiness, arguments, procrastination and other behaviors that can annoy and tire parents. Setting a child's routine is no small accomplishment. I commonly see parents of teenagers who are still struggling with where and when their teenager will sleep, eat and bathe.

I remember a six-year-old girl who had been referred because of behavior problems at school. In the process of getting routine information about the family, I learned the girl always slept in the den on the sofa, rather than in her bedroom. Her mother explained the daughter liked to go to sleep watching TV in the den and cried if the mother tried to make her sleep in her own bed. The parents decided it was less trouble to let their daughter stay in the den than trying to convince her to go to her room. The mother was perplexed when I said this behavior should be confronted and she asked, "What difference does it make where you sleep, if you sleep?"

Later that day, I saw another patient whose behavior answered that question. A seventeen-year-old boy had slipped out of his house and spent the night at his girlfriend's, unbeknownst to her parents. When I questioned this behavior, his response was, "What difference does it make where you sleep, as long as you sleep?"

Teaching children manners also helps them to show respect for others. Some parents feel manners are old fashioned and outdated. However, manners will never hurt a child. The same cannot be said for rude and disrespectful behavior. The Bible says that this can be recognized at a young age. Proverbs 20: 11, *"Even small children are known by their actions, so is their conduct really pure and upright?"*

Parents should not permit a child to be verbally disrespectful to them or any adult. Calling parents or grandparents degrading names, even in a playful fashion, is not helpful, as children have difficulty understanding this is less acceptable when they get older. Children should never hit their parents. Even infants can understand that hitting parents is not acceptable. Proverbs 19:26 says, *"A son who mistreats his father or mother is a public disgrace.*

DEFIANCE

Confronting a child's defiance will become increasingly more difficult as the child ages. It is much easier to teach a child you are more powerful, if you are. Contrast how you might manage a three-year-old child who spits in your face to a seventeen-year-old child who spits in your face. Parents too easily ignore or deny their child's disobedient and disrespectful behavior. Parents of the "Now Generation" may become accustomed to getting what they want immediately. If their child's honor and respect does not come quickly and easily, some parents abandon the effort to deal with this problem.

It may take years and hundreds of struggles with a particularly strong-willed child before the parents can establish their authority. These conflicts are an opportunity to teach your child to respect authority, while you still have the power and control. When reprimanding your children, insist they look you in the eyes, listen to you and acknowledge they understand and accept your authority. No matter how unpleasant, time consuming and difficult this teaching seems when he or she is young, it will never get easier. It is natural for young children to question their parents' authority. However, there is a difference between listening to children in order to understand and teach them, and allowing children to ignore and/or defy parents. As children's personalities develop there will be times when the conflict between what children want, and parental limits, will escalate into children becoming defiant. Both from a psychiatric and a Biblical perspective, confronting child defiance is an essential feature of learning to respect authority.

Parents will never have their children's respect if they let the children defy them. Child rearing allows many opportunities for power struggles, arguing and children exerting their independence. However, blatant defiance by children should not be tolerated. "Defiance" means a child's behavior is out of control, parents cannot reason with the child and the child refuses to obey. Such situations generally occur in early childhood. Physical intervention may become necessary for the parent to protect the child or others, and to reestablish parental control. Often this can be done by holding or restraining the child. Sometimes spanking may be indicated.

SPANKING

In an adolescent psychotherapy group, I jokingly made the remark, "Santa might bring switches" to one of the group members. My comment was met by blank stares. None of the seven members knew a definition for the word other than the type of "switch" used to turn on an electric light or a computer. Few of my child and adolescent patients report they were ever spanked. The Bible says that spanking is an acceptable method for dealing with a child's defiance.

According to Proverbs 13:24, ***"He who spares the rod hates his son, but he who loves him is careful to discipline him."*** Similarly, Proverbs 22:15 states, ***"Folly is bound up in the heart of a child, but the rod of discipline will drive it far from him."***

There are parents who are so immature, so troubled and so unstable that they have neither the discernment nor self-control to safely use spanking as a method for teaching and protecting their children. However, these parents are not the majority. Our culture has come to classify all physical discipline, even that done by loving concerned parents, as being similar to the abusive, cruel behavior of the sociopath. Normal, loving parents do not spank a child to relieve their own frustrations. Such parents will take into account extenuating circumstances that may have led to a child's defiant behavior. With my rearing of six children, I can only remember two occasions when I spanked a child. However, our children knew that spanking was a possibility and the threat of the actual act was most times enough to establish control. Being physical with a young child on such rare occasions should be a loving and protecting act. It is not child abuse. It is painful for parents to have to resort to such measures. The old adage, "this is hurting me more than it is hurting you," reflects the proper state of mind for parents who must spank their child.

Keep in mind my thoughts on this matter are not universal. The American Academy of Family Physicians, American Academy of Pediatrics, American Association of Child & Adolescent Psychiatry, American Bar Association all have policies that condemn corporal punishment on children.

My view is that a slap on the hand may protect young children who do not understand consequences. It is certainly better for a child to learn running into the street will cause a spanking than to learn from being hit by a car. Scripture says it is permissible, and at times indicated; ***"Don't fail to correct your children; discipline won't hurt them! They won't die if you use a switch on them! Punishment will keep them out of hell"*** (Proverbs 23:13-14). The Old Testament touts the benefit of corporal punishment, but I could not find a place where Jesus recommended it. In the matter of corporal punishment, a parent must use common sense and take into consideration what authoritative sources have to say about the matter. A loving parent should make the decision about what is best for each individual child and circumstance.

The older the child, the less likelihood spanking should be used. It is particularly questionable to spank a child who has entered puberty. Although parents may perceive their young adolescents as children, adolescents have many adult feelings and can consider a spanking an assault. If your children require spanking, it should be administered rarely and only in their early years.

The Bible gives parents authority over their children and says parents are accountable to God should they misuse this trust. Jesus said in Matthew 18:6, *"But if any of you causes these little ones who trust in Me to lose his faith, it would be better for you to have a rock tied to your neck and be thrown into the sea."*

Governmental laws also hold parents responsible if they neglect or abuse a child. The parents' job is to teach their children to respect authority. God and the courts will take action should the parents abuse this power.

BEING BEST FRIENDS

Parents sometimes worry that being authoritative will cause their children to feel inferior and have low self-esteem. Discipline is not a self-esteem issue. Parents who treat their children like children are relating appropriately. It is a disservice to their children to do otherwise, as it denies the reality that there is a difference. Parents and children are not equal. Nowhere in the Bible are parents advised to be a friend of their child. A child does not recognize the authority of his/her friend. Being your child's best friend may prolong dependence on parents and make it more difficult for the child to develop a separate identity.

When a parent (usually the mother) considers her child (usually the daughter) her "best friend," it often also indicates there is an alliance exclusive of the other parent (usually the father). This is destructive to the parents' relationship with each other.

Adolescents who are too close to a parent may eventually have to use extraordinary effort to become independent. Acting out behaviors, such as outlandish physical appearance and dress, defiance, drug and alcohol use and sexual promiscuity, may be the only way the teenager knows to break away from a smothering parent. The degree of teenage rebellion sometimes seems linked to an abnormal degree of apparent closeness between a parent and child.

If your children enter kindergarten having firmly established an attitude of respect for their parents, they will be ready to devote their energies to learning, rather than struggling with teachers over authority issues that should have been already settled by parents. Children who honor their father and mother should adjust well to school, as they have been prepared to accept discipline.

CHAPTER NINE

DISCIPLINE AS LOVE

Discipline goes hand in hand with teaching children to honor their father and mother. Parents who are honored by their children spend less time and effort disciplining them. Similarly, their children will honor parents who use discipline lovingly. The book of Proverbs, written primarily by King Solomon, has been described as a guide for being successful in life. It contains many recommendations on how to parent a child. Solomon tells us the way a child is raised will define his personality and character as an adult. Solomon stressed the importance of disciplining children: *"Young man, do not resent it when God chastens and corrects you, for His punishment is proof of His love. Just as a father punishes a son he delights to make him better, so the Lord corrects you"* (Proverbs 3:11-12).

"Discipline your son in his early years while there is hope. If you don't, you will ruin his life" (Proverbs 19:18).

From the New Testament, Hebrews 12:7: *"Let God train you, for He is doing what any loving father does for his children. Whoever heard of a son who was never corrected?"* and Hebrews 12:11, *"Being punished isn't enjoyable while it is happening - it hurts! But afterwards we can see the result, a quiet growth in grace and character."*

PERMISSIVE PARENTING

Child psychiatrists have an undeserved reputation of encouraging permissive parenting. We, of all people, realize the great harm done to children whose parents do not discipline. These children frequently become our patients with symptoms of temper tantrums, defiance, rage, low frustration tolerance, depression, vandalism, criminality, poor school adjustment and drug use. According to the Bible and psychological theory, discipline is an essential feature of parent/child interaction. It should be administered as a part of parents' love for their child. God told John in Revelations 3:19, ***"I continually discipline and punish everyone I love."***

It has been my experience that adults, who seem the most consistently loving to others and who have the best relationship with their own parents, were raised in homes where discipline was clear, fair and firm. These adults do not look back on their childhood as harsh or abusive. They tell with amusement and fondness of times when they as children were disciplined by parents for bad behavior. There is a sense of pride in their parents and themselves for the lessons they learned. *Proverbs 29:17 says, **"Discipline your son and he will give you happiness and peace of mind."***

On the other hand, I have seen young children and adolescents who have not been disciplined, and they despise their parents. According to I Kings 1:6, King David's son, Adonijah, turned against his father because, ***"King David had never disciplined him at any time."***

CONSCIENCE AND CONSEQUENCES

Psychiatrists believe children may develop consciences from the way they are disciplined by their parents. When children mature, their parents remain in their unconscious minds ready to admonish them with guilt if they begin to do something wrong. It is ironic that some parents avoid punishing their children, feeling the children will identify with the parents' harshness and will grow up to be overly aggressive or violent adults. To the contrary, these parents may raise children who have little or no conscience, as commonly seen in cruel and unlawful adults.

Discipline, administered with love, is a tool parents should use to civilize their children and to prepare them for safe, successful lives after they leave home. Just as a cute little puppy without training will grow into an unruly and unwelcome adult animal, so may an adorable young child, without proper discipline, live an adult life of alienation and rejection. Discipline enables us to teach our children, in our safe and loving homes, that there are consequences for their actions.

Emotionally healthy children begin to experience discipline early in life. When an infant becomes excessively demanding and aggressive, like throwing a bottle down on the floor or having a tantrum, the mother shows her displeasure. She supports or rewards her child's behavior depending on her judgment of its appropriateness. This requires the mother to be comfortable with allowing some frustration of the infant. Her action clearly translates to the child that she is in control of their relationship.

This is the way discipline begins. Parents who themselves are insecure and fear criticism from a spouse or others, may have difficulty setting limits for their child. Also, parents who spend little time with their child may be reluctant to discipline, wanting their child to be happy during the relatively brief time parent and child are together.

If children honor and respect their parents, discipline is relatively easy. Children want to please their parents and are uncomfortable if their parents show disapproval. Punishment can be a facial expression, a gesture or words. As children get older, parents commonly punish by depriving the children of something the children enjoy. Common examples are grounding, being restricted to their room and no television. Such punishments are often ineffective, as they tend to be poorly thought out, unimaginative and repetitive.

DISCIPLINE SUGGESTIONS

Parents in my practice have demonstrated many helpful ways to discipline in a constructive and effective fashion. Some techniques they have found useful are:

1. When practical, let children learn from the natural consequences of their behavior. For example, rather than excessively arguing with children that they will need a coat to be warm, let the cold teach them this lesson.
2. Parents should avoid depriving children of an activity that is constructive. If children have trouble making friends, it is self-defeating to punish them by not letting them go to another child's birthday party or to baseball practice. If possible, a parent should take away activities that the parent does not particularly see as beneficial. Examples might be depriving them of watching television, or eating deserts.
3. It is more meaningful if the punishment can be related to the offense. If children abuse phone time, it is logical to ground them from the phone or remove the phone from their room. I know one parent who disciplines her children for not writing thank-you notes by taking away their present until the note is written. Other parents make their child give a toy to charity when their child is intentionally destructive. Taking toys away from children and returning them only after they keep their room tidy for a certain number of days is an example of this strategy.
4. Try having your children "do" rather than "not do" something as a punishment. Grounding and depriving children of something they like is the most frequent punishment that parents use. The penal system, notorious for being ineffective for correcting bad behavior, relies on a similar system. Teachers and coaches, however, often use action-based punishment to help children learn from their errors. Examples are having children run laps, do push ups or copy a sentence repeatedly. Parents can use similar techniques. Examples I have seen include having the

child clean the garage, wash windows, weed flowerbeds, paint, clean closets, polish shoes and wash the car. One parent had his son write a theme on the dangers of sneaking out at night.
5. Work that is used as punishment should be constructive. Children can write spelling words, do math problems, memorize Bible verses or do other intellectual work they tend to avoid. These punishments give the child a sense of accomplishment. The punishments should be in addition to, and not replace, routine chores.
6. Parents may avoid do-something discipline because it requires time and effort. It is much easier, in the short term, to send a child to his or her room or take away TV privileges than to monitor a constructive activity. Parents who use "do-something" discipline will need to enforce, instruct, direct and supervise their child's effort. The parent/child interaction involved in this process can be true quality time for your child.
7. Punishment should be used sparingly and wisely. Ephesians 6:4 says, ***"Don't keep on scolding and nagging your children, making them angry and resentful."*** Children may become defiant if the parents' discipline is blatantly unreasonable or too harsh. Parents who set punishments that are overly severe tend not to enforce them. The end result is a child who is less regularly disciplined.
8. Except in cases where a child is in serious danger of hurting himself or another person, parents should avoid administering punishment in public or in front of a child's friends. This may humiliate children so severely they will defy their parents.
9. After an upsetting conflict, it is usually best to delay giving punishment until you and/or the child have calmed down. Punishing children when they are already severely distraught can cause defiance. On the

other hand, if parent and child are in control, it is preferable to discipline a child soon after the act. Some children forget why they are being punished if discipline is too delayed.

10. No discipline should be used which children will not obey or which the parents cannot enforce. I may advise parents to hold back from punishing a child when it is clear the parents do not have, or do not want to use, the power to enforce their discipline. For example, it is ludicrous to use grounding as a punishment when a teenager regularly defies the parents by leaving home without permission.

11. Parents who have not spent much time with their children may not have enough information to make sound judgments about discipline. This can cause discipline to be confused, inconsistent and unwisely administered. Small matters can escalate into severe crises that can have unhealthy effects on a family. Parents should be consistent in the way they discipline. Good communication between parents promotes consistent discipline and decreases the likelihood of the child avoiding punishment by playing one parent against the other.

12. Punishment should not require children to enforce the consequences of their behavior upon themselves. For example, parents sometimes ground children from watching TV and then let them spend the night with a friend. Most children do not have the maturity to inform friends they are restricted from TV. Instead, children will disobey their parents and go ahead and watch TV and then lie about what they did at their friend's house. It would have been better for the parents to limit children's TV time at home only.

Discipline is only one way a child's personality is shaped. The impact of parents being positive role models for their children has already been emphasized. Reward of a child's positive behavior is also very important. Although children understand there are consequences if they are bad, they seldom appreciate that their privileges will increase when they are good. It is helpful if parents verbalized this connection. Examples might include: "You have been so helpful and obedient this week, why don't you invite a friend to go to the movie with us tonight?" or "You have been keeping your room so neat, I would like to get a new bedspread for you." or "You have been so polite recently, I would like to do something special with you." There are repeated examples in the Bible where individuals, cities and nations are rewarded for their devotion to God and good works. Children can benefit from a similar program.

The Bible does not instruct us how to reward or punish children in specific situations. There are numerous secular books on child rearing that discuss specific methods and techniques: James Dobson's (Note 4) book, <u>The New Dare to Discipline</u>, provides a particularly useful Christian perspective. God holds parents responsible for providing discipline for their children.

Humans also judge us by how we manage our family. Paul wrote in 1 Timothy 3:4 a pastor must *"have a well behaved family with children who obey quickly and quietly. For if a man can't make his own little family behave, how can he help the whole church?"* Like it or not, how parents control their children is considered a reflection of how well they manage other aspects of their lives. Loving discipline is a missing ingredient in many homes today. Putting discipline back into child rearing is psychologically healthy and Biblically sound. Some parents rely too heavily on educating their children to make the right choice. Education alone is not the answer.

CHAPTER TEN

EDUCATION IS NOT THE ANSWER

In II Chronicles 1:11-12, God said to Solomon, *"Because your greatest desire is to help your people, and you haven't asked for personal wealth and honor, and you haven't asked Me to curse your enemies, and you haven't asked for a long life, but for wisdom and knowledge to properly guide My people - yes, I am giving you the knowledge and wisdom you asked for! And I am also giving you such riches, wealth, and honor as no other king has ever had before you! And there will never again be so great a king in all the world!"*

Can you imagine the satisfaction and sense of well being his parents, King David and Bathsheba, must have felt watching Solomon grow into a man? If ever a man would be able to make the right choices, it would be their son Solomon, the most knowledgeable man in the world. Unfortunately, even a wise man may choose to be disobedient. Even though Solomon well understood the consequences of ungodly behavior, he drank excessively, womanized, became egotistical and cynical. Solomon, the wisest man on earth, spent much of his later life disillusioned and in despair. (Ecclesiastes 2:20-23).   If knowledge could not protect a Solomon from making self-destructive choices, we should not count on knowledge being adequate protection for our children. Moses in Deuteronomy 4:9-10 tells parents to teach their children to *"know God's miracles, to fear God, and to learn His laws."* The Bible does not say to educate children and then let them make their own decisions.

"Teaching your child to make the right choices" has become a guiding principle for today's parents. In my opinion, over reliance on children being taught to make the right choices is often misguided and sometimes dangerous. Parents can expose their children to increased risk when they assume what children learn will protect them. This can happen when parents and educators teach children, "just say no" to riding with strangers, sex, alcohol, and drugs, instead of adequately supervising them. Although it is reasonable to work toward educating children to make safe decisions, it is foolhardy to think youngsters will regularly have enough discernment to protect themselves.

Children can learn a concept before they have the maturity or self-control to use it. For example, four-year- olds may understand if they go out of their yard, they may be harmed. Despite this knowledge, they may impulsively dart into the street. Some concepts require maturity before a child can actually put what is learned into practice. Most children do not understand that death is permanent until they are about eight years old. Parents certainly cannot rely on children knowing they can be killed as deterrent if the children do not appreciate that death is final.

Often children's "right choice" is influenced more by their respect and fear of punishment from parents than by knowledge about the dangerous consequences of behavior. I asked a teenage boy, after he had seen a film of an accident caused by speeding in which both the driver and his girlfriend were killed, if he would speed. He responded, "No way, man! If I got a speeding ticket, my parents would take the car away."

Children may follow the example of their parents, regardless of what others teach them. Lectures to a son on being respectful to women may be ineffective if he has a chauvinistic father. Children with few moral values make different decisions than those who have strong consciences. A conscience is a very useful part of a child's personality. Previous teaching of parents transforms in their children's minds into a conscience. It causes a child to automatically resist bad or dangerous behavior in order to avoid a feeling of guilt. There is nothing psychologically or Biblically wrong with children doing what is right, simply because it makes them feel better.

Research in brain chemistry has shown that drugs and/or alcohol trigger pleasure and reward signals that can overpower the judgment and common sense functions of the cerebral cortex. No matter how smart children are, their choices, like adults' choices, are different when they are under the influence of drugs and alcohol. The great danger of children and adolescents using drugs and alcohol can not be overstated. If when evaluating a disturbed, out of control, inadequate, miserable young adult I found that he came from a healthy loving family, almost always the underlying problem was drugs or alcohol. Drugs and alcohol use can throw years of positive parenting out the window. If nothing seems to work in managing your child, reconsider unsuspected drug or alcohol abuse.

The right choice for a child is also determined by the attractiveness of the temptation and by the setting. A boy will understand the risks of sneaking out, consistently turn down invitations to do it, and then go if a special person asks him. A girl may have been taught the consequences of having sex, resolve to remain a virgin until marriage, and yet give in if she is spending the night at a hotel party and has been drinking. Some situations have more appeal to certain individuals than to others. A underage teenager with a high genetic predisposition for alcoholism may have more difficulty avoiding alcohol than a child without a family history of alcoholism.

Children are highly influenced by peer pressure. Smoking is a good example. Children usually are well informed about the dangers of smoking. If parents smoke, their child may beg them to give up cigarettes. The same child, however, may succumb to peer pressure when offered a cigarette by a friend. Trying to stop smoking is an excellent example of the futility of relying on education alone to assure a child's right choices. Why do millions of adults who are fully educated about the hazards of smoking continue to smoke? If education about the risks of a particular act does not stop adults, then why should we rely on education to control children's behavior? The problem is not that children don't know better, it is that they either cannot or do not want to stop.

Children's emotional state will influence their choices. Children with attention deficit disorder (ADD) are impulsive and often act before thinking, even if they have fully learned and understood the consequences. Teenagers, and even young children, may suffer from depression. A child's mood will affect the ability to use information he or she has learned.

Teenagers' appreciation of risk will be weakened by a belief they are beyond harm, a common adolescent idea. Even after losing friends in automobile accidents, teenagers may continue to drink and drive recklessly. They understand the risk, but they don't see it as applicable to themselves. One adolescent group had a beer party in honor of their friend who died while driving intoxicated.

THE RESPONSIBILITY TO PROTECT

Few children can cope with today's complicated, sinful and dangerous life circumstances without some control and guidance of attentive parents. It is discouraging to watch program planners repeatedly turn to more education for children to avoid sexual abuse, practice safe sex or drive safely. Having children make an "A" in a course on driving safety, drug and alcohol abuse or teenage pregnancy, does not mean that parents don't have to protect them.

It is certainly easier in the short run to teach children the consequences and then let them look out for themselves. Parents must guard against responding to peer pressure and letting their children be unsupervised because "other parents are doing it." Parents must be careful about transferring too much responsibility for their children to others, or to the children themselves. Parents justifying providing less supervision because they are "helping their child learn to be independent" can be a dangerous.

WHEN TO LET GO

Successful parents protect their children to whatever degree is necessary until the children demonstrate an ability to surely make choices that are safe. This requires parents to make thousands of judgments that will affect the course of their children's lives. The parents must take into consideration the maturity of the child, as well as the likelihood and the severity of the risk. To do this, they must truly know and understand the level of their children's intelligence, judgment, self-control, mood and the way they are influenced by others. This means the parent must know their child's friends and have some idea about the friends' values and behavior. The parents must have information on planned activities and appreciate what risk each presents. The parent can then decide what level of responsibility will be given to the children and how much protection will be necessary. The choices parents make will largely determine how safely and successfully the child reaches adulthood.

Children should continually be given the opportunity to master new tasks and to handle responsibility. Each time children face and overcome a difficult or dangerous situation; they become wiser, stronger and more competent. However, parents must dish out these opportunities in bites their children can safely and successfully chew. As the child gets older, the parents' ability to correctly make these calls for their children is a hallmark of good parenting.

The process is analogous to coaching a rookie quarterback in the NFL. You can't just teach him the plays and send him onto the field. In addition to the teaching, he must practice under the scrutiny and support of his coach. He will be allowed limited playing time, under relatively controlled circumstances, such as playing him initially against teams known to have a weaker pass rush. Only when he has demonstrated repeated evidence of his competency is the rookie given more free rein. Putting him onto the field just because he understands the game plan would endanger him. The same is true for today's children. Like the NFL quarterback, a child will eventually reach a level of maturity which will allow more responsibility for making his or her "own choices.

David, in the 23rd Psalm, referred to the Lord as, ***"his Shepherd who provides for him, leads him to be righteous, and protects him from danger."*** I have little personal experience with sheepherders. However, I know that herding teenagers can seem to be a thankless task. Teenagers seem a lot less appreciative and more recalcitrant than sheep. Few appreciate or agree with their parents' caution. Protecting and managing teenagers will reinforce the importance of those years teaching them to honor and respect their parents.

Teenagers, in a relatively short time (about age 24 when their brains show evidence of adult maturity), will understand and appreciate their parents limits. Until then, they will need some shepherding. Shepherds during Jesus' time were not people of wealth. If shepherds were wealthy, wouldn't they hire someone else to care for the sheep so they could go into town? Wealth could lessen their motivation for shepherding. Being wealthy could be perilous for their sheep.

CHAPTER ELEVEN

THE PERILS OF WEALTH

Surprisingly, a family vacation can be an unhappy time for some families. The scenario goes like this. It might occur when affluent parents have previously provided expensive, elaborate mini-vacations for their family. On this particular summer, the parents decide to spend the family vacation in a modest cabin in the mountains. The children complain from the beginning about the trip. They say the parents are mean because they have not arranged for the children to bring a friend with them. They don't like having to wait at the airport and complain the drive in the rental car is too long. They resent having to wait while the parents buy groceries. They say the cabin is too hot, and they don't want to share a room with a sibling. The remainder of the week they whine, grumble, and try to make their parents miserable for bringing them on such a "boring" trip.

However, it is not their children's attitudes or behavior that discourages the parents, as they have grown accustomed to their children's rudeness, it is the way the family members are treating each other in Cabin 2. Each family member in Cabin 2 had saved and made some sacrifice to have this trip. Making plans together for it had been exciting for all of them. The children are respectful to their parents and clearly appreciate being able to enjoy such a wonderful family vacation. It is the contrast between the children in the two cabins that has discouraged the parents in Cabin 1. They realize something is wrong.

Working together to overcome financial hardship can promote consideration for others and build protective family alliances. Wealthy families can have so many opportunities for individual stimulation and excitement that strong family bonds may become less important. Family members are able to do their "own thing" with little consideration for the rest of the family. This may produce children who are self-centered and have less family loyalty. Wealth has its disadvantages. According to the Bible, wealth won't help you into Heaven: ***"For a soul is far too precious to be ransomed by mere earthly wealth. There is not enough of it in all the earth to buy eternal life for just one soul to keep it out of Hell"*** (Psalms 49:8-9).

"Then Jesus said to His disciples, 'It is almost impossible for a rich man to get into the Kingdom of Heaven. I say it again - It is easier for a camel to go through the eye of a needle than for a rich man to enter the Kingdom of Heaven'" (Matthew 19:23-24).

Wealth can corrupt us and make us less responsive to God's Word. When wealth induces parents to ignore God's directions in the Bible, wealth becomes a handicap to their children.

The Bible says that after Jesus was born Joseph offered a sacrifice of two turtle doves instead of the usual sacrifice of a lamb (Luke 2:24). Mosaic law permitted this substitution if the parents were poor. Joseph was a carpenter, and Mary was not a working mother. The parents God chose for Jesus were not wealthy. I assume God felt this was to His Son's advantage.

Having wealth does not automatically prevent a parent from raising a mentally healthy child. There are advantages for children of parents who do not have to worry about money. One very important benefit is the mother does not need to work, allowing her more time to protect, nurture, and influence her children. Affluence should also result in the father being more available to his family.

On the other hand, wealthy parents have attractive options such as travel, education, entertainment, housekeepers and nannies, which make it easier for them to spend less time with their children as they pursue more self-satisfying activities. Wealthy parents may become accustomed to and demand "quality" in their life experiences. While spending so much energy in a search for the best life has to offer, they can become pampered and spoiled. Self-indulgent parents tend to raise self-indulgent children.

OVER-INDULGED CHILDREN

Wealthy children may be so indulged there is little motivation for them to compete in the outside world. A nine-year-old boy was referred to me because he did not socialize. His domain was an entire wing of a mansion. He had the best entertainment equipment, video games, remote control cars, computers and toys at his fingertips. He had a tennis court, tennis coach and a swimming pool. Why should he socialize? He did not see the point.

All his needs and wishes were met at home and everything else seemed a step down. Only after extensive counseling were the parents able to limit his toys and provide sufficient pressure and incentives to cause him to leave his luxurious surroundings to play with other children.

When children become accustomed to having all their entertainment provided by their parents, they may abandon play that requires effort. They may dislike sports and other activities that require exercise. This causes them to have less in common with their classmates. Their interpersonal relationships may be affected as they exert minimal energy to make or keep friends.

The parents may try to compensate by providing expensive toys to draw friends or by inviting other children on elaborate trips. Such children may appear happy, well liked or even sophisticated in situations orchestrated by their parents, but can seem uncertain and immature when in social situations not arranged by their parents. Affluence allows parents and children to avoid activity that is uninteresting and monotonous. These parents hire others to mow the yard, wash the car, make the bed, clean the house, wash clothes or cook. The wealthier they become, the more work can be avoided.

There are few family work projects or chores for wealthy children. The parents' emphasis may become providing entertainment. These children see their parents living a life of luxury, never appreciating that their parents obtained this luxury by effort. Affluent children may seldom see the strengths of their parents' personalities that permitted the parents to become successful and gain wealth.

It can be detrimental for their children if the parents, intending to minimize "non-quality" time with their children, avoid the mundane side of parenting. This can result in the total time with their children significantly decreasing. Car pools being delegated to nannies or housekeepers will cause the parents and children to miss an opportunity for quality time.

HAVING THEIR OWN MONEY

Some children have had their own bank account since birth. Through childhood and adolescence, money received as gifts are placed into their accounts. It is courteous and also lessens irresponsible spending if a child writes the giver of the money to thank them and tell them how the money will be used. When children have their own money, it should be clear from the onset that the parents will control how it is spent. Children often assume that having their own money means they can spend the money however they choose.

When children have their own money, parents sometimes permit them to buy or do something that the parents would normally not approve. For example, a parent may not want a child to have a TV in his/her room but will allow it when the child uses his or her "own money." Thereafter parents may be reluctant to use grounding from TV as a punishment because it was bought with the child's own money.

The same scenario occurs with cell phones, iPods, CDs and concert tickets. If a child is allowed to withdraw money impulsively and spend it foolishly, it defeats the purpose of having a savings account. Parents are sometimes surprised to learn the money in the account may legally be the child's own money. Wealthy grandparents may avoid inheritance taxes by making monetary gifts to grandchildren each year for a college fund.

Under the Uniform Transfers to Minors Act (Note 5) this money must be given to the child when he or she becomes an adult (depending on the individual state, this could be set at eighteen or twenty-one years of age). The parents and grandparents can only hope the children decide to use this money for college. There is the possibility that some children will use their school money for activities that will stunt rather than promote growth.

TOO MUCH PRIVACY

Affluent families can provide each child with his/her own bedroom. Who can say whether this is good or bad? Learning to be civil and considerate while sharing a room with a sibling may provide a positive lesson for children. Children who have a bedroom to themselves can become possessive and territorial about their room. Parents describe how their children tell them, "Get out of my room!" or "Never go into my room without asking!" I have had parents tell me they are reluctant to confront their child about marijuana they found because the child will know they have been in his or her room.

Parents lose a danger deterrent when they decide not to enter a child's room. Children who know that their parents may come into their room are unlikely to hide drugs or alcohol there. Parents who regularly are in their child's room have assurance no uninvited guest is sleeping there. Room cleanliness and child study habits cannot be monitored through a closed door. When parents feel they cannot go into their children's rooms, privacy is being given excessive consideration.

CHILDREN WHO ARE BORED

Overindulged children frequently complain of boredom. Wealthy parents, who are making freedom from boredom an important goal in their own lives, don't want their children to be bored either. Parents may search for new and more exciting ways to stimulate and entertain them. Parents must resist being drawn into the children's perpetual "feel good" frenzy.

Children's wants will become increasingly more elaborate and expensive as they age. By the time some children of indulgent parents are seniors in high school, they have owned several new cars, dined in the finest restaurants, traveled extensively abroad, been accompanied by their friends to extravagant resorts and routinely bought themselves expensive clothes and toys. It becomes a challenge for them and their parents to find something not boring to do. It is a sign something is wrong when children regularly complain they are bored. Parents should be able to find constructive tasks or chores for children who complain of boredom.

When my wife and I married, blending two families, our teenage children were not excited about the modest cottage we planned to remodel for our new home. They wanted a "two story." When construction began, we made the children work with us on the weekend to clean the building site. They complained we were unfair. Soon their involvement in this family work program began to improve their attitude about our home. Over the months of construction, the complaining stopped, and they began to show friends their future home with pride.

Enforcing this project was not particularly fun for my wife or me. Often we said, "Why go to this trouble?" and "This is too much work." We could have had the contractor keep the job site clean or could have hired someone to clean it. That would have been a mistake. Most of us would like to avoid the tiresome, repetitious, difficult and sometimes unpleasant confrontations we have with our children as we teach them. We would thankfully take an easier way - if it were available. Wealthy parents have the resources to avoid much of the nitty-gritty of raising children.

The problems discussed in this chapter are not limited to the extremely rich. The negative impact of affluence is a factor in most American homes; it is a matter of degree. Many of the luxuries given to children of wealth can also be provided to families of moderate means. However, for the wealthy, how much something costs is not a deterrent, so parents and children are more often presented with unhealthy choices that are difficult to resist. Parents who are less wealthy just have fewer opportunities to make the same bad judgments.

Even if they can afford to, parents should be careful about giving in to their child's every wish. The goal is for parents to prepare their children to be successful adults, not to just keep them happy during childhood.

USEFUL SUGGESTIONS

The following are some ways I have seen wealthy parents protect their children from the perils of wealth:

1. Limit the number of toys you give your child. Children who have an overabundance of toys have a greater tendency to be unappreciative and wasteful. Try to buy some toys and games that you can play with your children.
2. Do not allow your children's' birthday parties to become too elaborate. Limit the number of gifts given. Some years have your child's party only include immediate family and grandparents.
3. Avoid regularly buying small trinkets and special treats for your child. The whining, begging, power struggles which occur in grocery lines between children and their parents should motivate you to not start this habit.

4. Limit the amount of time children play video games. Some parents allow children only two-player games in order to encourage interaction with others.
5. Do not equip your child's room for entertainment. Overindulged children may have a computer, television, telephone, and video games in their room. This encourages them to isolate themselves in their room, lessening involvement with the family. Also, for such children, being "grounded to their room" has less power as a deterrent or punishment.
6. Do not regularly provide a driver for your child. Driving time with children can be used to establish better communication; it may be one of the few times when child and parent have uninterrupted time together. If parents take their children to their activities they are more aware of what their child is doing.
7. Limit the use of cellular phones until the child has the maturity to use them. Cellular phones can be a disadvantage for parent/child communication. It is common to observe parents driving and talking on the phone while their child sits ignored. Furthermore, cell phones facilitate both parents and children being less accountable. With a cell phone, a parent may feel it is less important to control where their children are, because the parent can always get in touch with them. On the other hand, children are relieved they do not have to tell their parents where they are going, as parents are not able to call a specific location to check on them. Enforcing a phone curfew is more difficult with a cell phone. The result can vary from little problems, such as children not getting enough sleep because they are making or receiving late phone calls, to big problems, such as "sext messaging" or making drug contacts.
8. A home security system should have a control panel in the master bedroom. This alerts the parents if a door or

window is opened during the night. Such a system is of great help in keeping children in, as well as keeping burglars out.
9. If you give children everything they want with no effort required by them, they may not learn there is a direct relationship between work and gain. Some teenagers truly believe what one gets depends on how much they wish for it. As one teenager said, "It's not fair! She got a new car when I wanted one much more than she did."
10. Don't give children gifts that they don't have the maturity to use or appreciate. By the time some children become sixteen years old, they may have been given so much, the parents have exhausted ways to excite them. These parents may eagerly anticipate buying their child a car, sometimes the only thing for which the child has had to wait. I have seen parents buy their child a car a year before the child is legally able to drive. Is it surprising these children sometimes sneak their cars out?

Wealth sometimes permits parents to continue in a destructive course of child rearing for a period longer than would occur if the parents were not wealthy. Wealthy parents are harder to put back on track. Wealth brings power, so friends, relatives and doctors may be hesitant to confront wealthy parents to tell them they are neglecting or mismanaging their child. Even if approached, some wealthy parents are not receptive to such criticism and dismiss it as being said from jealousy.

Wealthy parents can raise their children to be fine people. However, it requires parents who have the self-discipline to stay actively involved in child rearing and not delegate parenting to others. Parents will need to exercise restraint to not overindulge their children. They should have them earn special purchases and activities. They must teach their children the value of hard work, even though the parents may have reached a point in their lives where they can largely avoid it.

It can be particularly helpful if wealthy parents study the Bible. I Timothy 6:10 says, ***"For the love of money is the first step toward all kinds of sin. Some people have even turned away from God because of their love for it, and as a result have pierced themselves with many sorrows."***

The road to being a good parent is paved by living a Godly life. The Bible gives guidance that is universal and can help parents see through some of the illusions created by wealth.

Attending church and Sunday school can also bring balance into the lives of affluent families. Church promotes awareness and giving to others who have less. In short, wealthy parents need to manage their children the way they would if they were not so wealthy. It is not easy to do. Ironically, some gain material wealth to do more for their children, only to find it causes them to do less.

Wealth creates many attractive, but unhealthy options for parents and children. Parents may entertain their children and their children's friends in increasingly extravagant and permissive ways, never realizing that they may be undermining their, and other parents' child-rearing efforts. This commonly occurs during a sleepover.

CHAPTER TWELVE

SABOTAGING PARENTING WITH SLEEPOVERS

A "sleepover" is when a child spends the night with a friend away from home. For many families sleepovers are regular events. A parent of a popular girl told me, "During the summer we try to have one night a week when she is either not over at a friend's house or has someone spending the night with her." Some parents use the quantity and quality of sleepovers to measure their child's social success. A sleepover has become a status symbol. There are parents who bring their children to me for psychiatric evaluation because their children are not invited to sleepovers.

On the surface sleepovers may seem to be beneficial for a young child, or certainly not harmful. They appear to be opportunities for young children to begin to safely separate from their parents and become more independent. Sleepovers should improve children's social skills. They permit respite for the parents who want a weekend break from the responsibilities of being a parent. Some children are mature enough that exposure to a different lifestyle in other homes is not damaging and may complement their positive feelings about their own families.

However, when a child is emotionally fragile or when the host family is dysfunctional, parents put their children at risk. In either case, when sleepovers continue into a child's teenage years, parents may rue the day they started them. Thirty years of treating adolescent patients has taught me that a high percentage of DWIs (driving while intoxicated), MIPs (minor in possession), drug overdoses, teenage pregnancies, injuries, acts of vandalism and deaths of teenagers happen when teenagers spend the night away from home. Parents would save themselves and their children a lot of grief if they break their child's sleepover habit or, even better, never let it begin.

WHAT'S WRONG WITH SLEEPOVERS?

It is easy for parents to be convinced that sleepovers are harmless, if not positive. However, there are good reasons to limit them:

1. Parents unknowingly, may be putting too much emphasis on entertaining children. Children come to expect exciting entertainment each weekend and blame their parents if they can't have it. Worse, it can imply that to be entertained, it is best to be away from your parents.
2. Letting children regularly stay away from home can insidiously tear down their respect for their own parents. Children will not want to stay home because there is "nothing to do."
3. Children spending nights away from home interrupts the routine that families today have such difficulty establishing. Usually the host family eliminates or slackens their rules about bedtime, phone calls, and TV, as they don't want the visitor to think they and their child is not "cool." Children usually come home from a sleepover exhausted and irritable. Children whose parents monitor their TV shows are always eager to visit a home where there is late night access to violent and sexual movies. It becomes increasingly difficult for these children to accept and be reintegrated into the routine of their own home.
4. Sleepovers foster the idea that it is not good for a child to have time alone. Some children have little opportunity to learn to entertain themselves.
5. On a sleepover, young children often are permitted privileges that are beyond what is appropriate for their

age. This is done because it is a "special occasion." The problem is these special occasions come every weekend and even more frequently in the summer. One example is when the host parents take their children and friends to rock concerts. Parents who do not usually permit their children to attend a rock concert will give in and let them go because they are at a sleepover.

6. There are more overt problems that can occur during a sleepover. If there is not adequate supervision, elementary grade children may engage in sexual play. Children in this day and time often are shockingly knowledgeable about sexual acts. Sex play today may involve oral sex and other sexual activity that would have been unknown to young children twenty years ago. Irate parents will discover their child has engaged in sexual activity while at a friend's home and uproar ensues. Parents may not have enough knowledge about the host parents to be confident that they are responsible people. Unfortunately, even this is no guarantee. Parents may invite a child for a sleepover and then have a baby-sitter or an older sibling stay with the children, introducing another unknown and potential risk factor.

7. Parents who implement the child rearing principles of the Bible are not in the majority. If children spend two days a week in homes where the lifestyle and value system is contrary to their own, it can undermine the other five days of parental effort. The attractiveness of a more exciting and stimulating life at a friend's house can make living a moral life of moderation seem even less appealing.

8. There may be subtle differences in parenting styles that eventually can erode the children's confidence in their own parents. For example, some parents may feel it is cute to take young children out after-hours to let

them wrap a house like the older kids. This is not the end of the world, but will be harmful if children are continually exposed to influences contrary to their parents' values.

9. Parents cannot control or fully appreciate what goes on in another child's home. A fourteen-year-old boy, raised in a family that practices many of the child rearing principles in this book, after much begging convinced his parents to let him go on a sleepover. At one o'clock in the morning the two boys were in the bedroom making prank telephone calls. The visitor, raised in a home where no guns had ever been present, playfully pointed a pistol that was loaded at his friend. Only God's providence kept him from pulling the trigger.

10. Sleepovers can cause children to become over invested in the importance of friends. Friends may encourage a teenager to defy parental guidelines and discard values that parents have spent years establishing. If parents support the view that the most important thing in their life is to have friends, children may come to feel the opinions of friends take precedence over those of their parents. Teenagers, without adult input, guiding other teenagers, are like the blind leading the blind.

WHY DO PARENTS ENCOURAGE SLEEPOVERS?

Parents may let sleepovers continue because they don't realize teenagers generally want to be away from home to get away from the control and supervision of their parents. Sometimes a sleepover is primarily a ploy to prevent parents from knowing where they are and what they are doing. Teenagers may set up a series of false locations, making it difficult to track them. Each parent thinks their child is staying at another house when in fact the teenagers are at a location where there are no parents.

Parents may find themselves powerless to deny teenagers a sleepover when it has been routine since early childhood. Parents are so sensitive to social pressure; they may not prohibit sleepovers because the parents are afraid other parents will criticize them. The parents themselves may have things they prefer to do and enjoy the relief from taking responsibility for their troublesome teenager. Having their child away on a sleepover can give parents a misconception that some other parent is in control.

It takes courage for parents to stick by their convictions and do what is right, rather than what is popular or easy. I feel sleepovers should rarely be permitted during elementary school, only on special occasions and under controlled conditions. I see no useful purpose for teenager sleepovers.

My advice is to simplify your lives, ration children's sleepovers carefully and use the limited time you have with your children, protecting and guiding them. As a shepherd with your flock, you cannot watch over your children when they are not with you. The shepherd does not allow his sheep to sleep elsewhere.

Frequent sleepovers can cause parents to have less confidence in their judgment about their children's behavior. Parents may become uncertain whether a child's behavior is the result of family interaction, a variant of normal development, or something the child was exposed to when he/she were on a sleepover. This becomes particularly a problem if parents are divorced.

CHAPTER THIRTEEN

DIVORCE AND CHILD CUSTODY

The Bible says that God intends marriage to be for life. In Romans 7:3, Paul writes, *"when a woman marries, the law binds her to her husband as long as he is alive."* In Mark 10:7-9, Jesus says, *"from the very first He made man and woman to be joined together permanently in marriage; therefore, a man is to leave his father and mother, and he and his wife are united so that they are no longer two, but one. And no man may separate what God has joined together."* In I Corinthians 7:14, Paul says that even if just one of the parents is a Christian, they should not separate because, *"the children might never come to know the Lord; whereas a united family, in God's plan, results in the children's salvation."*

With so many marriages ending in divorce, we have moved far from God's instructions. Couples often marry without appreciating that their vows are a covenant with God and their unborn children, not only to their spouse. A vow to God should not be taken lightly. How many parents literally give their promise to God much consideration when they decide to divorce? If God is an integral part of a marriage, shouldn't He be at least consulted through prayer when considering a divorce?

Raising a child alone without the observations, judgment, support and assistance of a mate can be a painful handicap. Parents rationalize the children will be better off if they are not living in a family with two unhappy parents. Although some adults seem to be more fulfilled after leaving a spouse, this is rarely true for their children. Most children continue to hope their parents will reconcile, and their family will be together again. Parents seldom appreciate the pain children experience during a divorce. Children feel their parents' anger. When parents directly or indirectly devalue their ex-spouse, the child also feels the barb.

When children live in the battle zone of a divorce, they dread occasions when their parents are together. Parents who scream, curse, slam doors, break objects and drive recklessly when angry, can terrify a child. Children may appear preoccupied, dazed and confused as they try to shut out the pain and suffering of seeing the parents they love tear into each other. The regular exposure of a child to such conflict can erode a child's emotional health and block future personality development.

Fortunately, children are resilient and can recover from even severe parental conflict if it is of brief duration. Children cannot withstand years of inconsistency, fear, manipulation, rage, sorrow, uncertainty and/or violence that sometimes continues even after parents are divorced.

Children are at the mercy of their parents' judgment and behavior. Consider this situation. A nine-year-old boy is in the custody of his mother and stepfather. The boy's baseball team is playing its championship game on Saturday. The natural father comes into town with his new wife and is eager to go to the game. The two sets of parents do not have the tolerance or self-control to discuss an arrangement that will allow both to attend without incident. It is likely, if both parents and their new spouses go to the game, there will be an angry scene.

For the child's sake, one of the fathers must give up his right to be at the child's baseball game. If the mother and stepfather will not compromise, then the natural father should not attend. The pleasure and benefit his son will gain from having his natural father in the stands is outweighed by the emotional pain, the boy would feel, should his two dads get into a fistfight.

WHO GETS CUSTODY?

In I Kings 3:17-27, Solomon ordered a child be cut in half and equal parts given to arguing mothers. When the biological mother offered to give the child to the other woman, he was able to identify her as the truly loving parent. Parents today often refuse to compromise their position, even if struggling with their ex-spouse is pulling the children apart emotionally.

Parents can become so determined that a child be influenced by their value system instead of their ex-spouse's, they may insist upon contact with the child regardless of the amount of conflict it creates.

Sometimes attorneys recommend that divorcing parents use a child psychiatrist as an expert witness. Parents and attorneys may have an unrealistic view of what can be accomplished through the use of psychiatric testimony. Both sides may find mental heath professionals who will support their position that the child should be placed in their client's custody. Having experts testify with different opinions from the same data can be disconcerting, inconclusive and expensive. A legal fight with multiple evaluations of the children, social studies and depositions will take a toll on children. Winning a court battle often is not worth the child casualties.

The most common custody arrangement is for one parent to be designated the managing conservator (the parent who has the child most of the time) and the other the possessing conservator (the parent who has the child every other weekend). Every other week, the children are required to have dinner one weekday with the possessing conservator. Such a schedule can disrupt the structure and consistency a child needs, and it provides another opportunity for conflict between the divorced parents. Even though both parents with this arrangement have frequent access to their children, the parent who is not with them may call regularly to tell the children that they love them. Such calls are usually unnecessary and may create anxiety for the children. Most often the need to maintain such frequent reassuring contact is the need of the parent, not the child.

Routinely the managing conservator (I will refer to as the mother, although it may be the father) has the ultimate authority over the child. She will decide where the child will go to school and church and which doctors will be used. Fathers often are angered by such an arrangement, because they find themselves with no control. Some parents who, while in a marriage seldom spent a weekend with their children, will go repeatedly to court after a divorce to obtain a few more hours.

It would be better if fathers stopped the legal haggling over the amount of days and hours they can spend with their children and instead come to an overall conclusion about what is best for their children and what they realistically can do about it. If the father knows the mother is damaging the children; if the father is sure he can provide a safer and more nurturing environment, if the father is advised by an attorney there is some chance of success in a court battle and if the father has ample funds and can afford the cost of a lengthy court battle, then he should sue for custody. Get it over with! Let the children have the benefit of consistency and freedom from conflict during the time that remains in their childhood.

However, if the father concludes the mother is not overtly damaging the children, if he cannot offer a clearly superior home for the children or if he cannot afford it and may not win in court, then he should accept his plight. The father should become reconciled to his relative lack of influence over his children's lives. His positive impact will be less if having more involvement with the children causes them continued conflict. He should simply try to be the best parent he can be and enjoy his children when he has them.

There will be more opportunities for the father to guide his children if he does not wage a continuous battle against the mother. If the father is reasonable, when the mother needs a break, she may ask the father to spend more time with the children.

JOINT CUSTODY

In my experience, joint custody with parents equally sharing responsibility for children usually is an unsatisfactory solution. If divorced parents can negotiate an arrangement that gives consideration to each of the parent's feelings and provides for the best interest of their children, then the parents are probably compatible enough to have saved their marriage. Parents who divorce each other are usually angry and distrustful of each other. It is the exception when they work in a cooperative, cordial fashion. In many instances, joint custody merely provides a mechanism for continuing conflict between the parents, and recurring trauma for the children.

If joint custody is chosen, I prefer children to have longer blocks of time with each parent. One satisfactory arrangement had the children spend one school semester with one parent and the second semester with the other. In the summer each parent had an uninterrupted six weeks with the children.

Sometimes children of divorced parents cannot tell me where they will be that night. Children who are uncertain about where they will sleep, who will pick them up from school or whether the person who takes them to scouts will be the same one to take them home, can be confused and insecure.

Denied the benefit of having routine in their lives, these children are at risk for emotional problems. Even when joint custody with equal time for each parent seems to work well, it has a limited period of usefulness. It becomes impractical for children to frequently move from one household to another when children are older and highly involved with school activities, friends and other interests.

SPLITTING SIBLINGS

The legal system and mental health workers do their best to provide alternatives that allow both parents to enjoy their children and influence their personality and values. What if no compromise can be reached and the parents doggedly persist in each having equal access, even though this causes continuing conflict and trauma for the children? Sometimes I propose that "split custody" be considered. Split custody is dividing siblings between two parents. Each parent would have a child for whom he/she is the managing conservator. Parents and judges frequently resist this suggestion. In my opinion, if splitting the children will avoid living in conflict, it is worth a try. There are specific situations when splitting custody has a distinct advantage. For example, splitting can provide a troubled child the attention and resources which would be unavailable if he or she had to share the parent with other brothers and sisters.

There is no Biblical writing that condemns separating siblings. Moses was raised separately from his siblings, yet in adulthood reestablished a close relationship with his brother Aaron (Exodus 4:27) and his sister, Miriam (Exodus 15:20). God instructed that Isaac and his half-brother, Ishmael, be separated and raised separately (Genesis 21:9- 14). If splitting children can protect them from parental warfare, then parents, professionals and judges should be more open to the concept. From my experience, the abhorrence of splitting siblings is not justified. Sometimes there is a good reason for them to be separated.

THE FRIENDLY DIVORCE

There are families who manage a divorce with less difficulty than has been described. Such exceptional parents are able to maintain a respectful, cooperative relationship with each other. They regularly communicate to assure their rules and values for their children remain consistent. Privileges, discipline and responsibilities are enforced equally at both homes. They will not use their children to deliver messages to each other, but communicate directly, preventing the child from distorting or manipulating.

Such parents never belittle or undermine their ex-spouse to their children. The parents do not vie for the approval of their children, causing the children to become entitled, manipulative and/or out-of-control. These parents are flexible in altering visitation patterns to accommodate the needs of both families. Each is satisfied with the other's financial contributions. They agree on or accept the other's choice of schools, church, camp and doctors. These parents exchange children from one family to the other in a cordial and helpful manner.

Parents who can conduct themselves with the self-control and consideration described above may permit their children to survive a divorce emotionally unscathed. Parents still must tackle raising their children alone, something that was designed to be a two-parent job. This can be done, but it will require exceptional skill, self-sacrifice, energy, courage, and divine help.

Providing a secure base for children while they grow into adulthood is essential. Parents must continually judge the degree of responsibility their children can safely assume. Because divorced parents' time with their children may not be continuous or consistent, making correct judgments about their children and providing needed control is more difficult, particularly if the parents undermine each other's efforts. Battling an angry ex-mate and a rebellious youngster can make parenting almost impossible. In these complex and difficult situations, psychiatric consultation can be helpful; but a miracle may be required. A good place to begin is to pray. See Chapter 10 of Part II entitled "Parent Praying."

Before transitioning into Part II, Parenting Messages From The New Testament, I will try to summarize the major points in Part I.

PART I - SUMMING UP

PRINCIPLES FOR CHILD-REARING:

1. Worship God. A strong spiritual life will lead to a loving and effective family life.
2. Marry for life. Parenting is meant to be a two-person job.
3. The most effective way to influence your children is to spend time with them and be a good example.
4. "Honor your father and mother." This is the basis for children developing respect for authority.
5. Discipline is part of love. Do not permit your children to be defiant.
6. Establish a routine for your children's bedtime, eating habits and personal hygiene before they are six years old.
7. Teach your children they are important because God loves them; confidence and self-esteem will follow.
8. A parent's love, like God's, should be forgiving but there should be consequences for bad behavior.
9. More "quality time" with children should not cause the "quantity" of time to decrease.
10. Limit sleep-overs to special occasions.
11. Seek opportunities for you and your children to pray together.
12. Raise your children in an environment where they will have other positive role models. Participate in church activities.
13. Make meals together a family routine and carefully protect this time.
14. Teaching children to "make the right choices" is no substitute for parental judgment and protection. Children can understand danger before they have the maturity to avoid it.

15. Know your children's friends, and activities, so you can judge when to protect, and when to let go.
16. Let home be a secure "base" for your children, but prepare them to safely move into the adult world.
17. Wealth creates special parenting challenges. Wealthy parents must be careful not to delegate the work of parenting.
18. If your goal is to raise children the way God would like, study God's parenting manual, the Bible.

PART II

PARENTING MESSAGES FROM THE NEW TESTAMENT

Parenting Messages from the New Testament highlights that there is much more to "growing up" than just learning to "follow the rules." The rules and commandments in the New Testament are more subtle than those in the Old Testament, which were mostly to help parents rear young children. Specific rules are more difficult when parents are dealing with teenagers and young adults who have varying and rapidly changing degrees of biological and theological maturity. Also, since older children have parts of their personality that are more similar to their adult parents, the guidelines seem to be written as much to the parents as to the children. Parents maintaining open communication with the Holy Spirit through prayer is important in finding the best way to apply these directions to an adolescent.

INTRODUCTION

In the New Testament, Jesus seems to expect that the Ten Commandments have been already written on our heart (Romans 2:15). The New Testament shows us God in the body and person of Jesus. When we identify Christ's attributes, we will see what we will need to be like when we join His family in Heaven. These same qualities will also smooth our adjustment on earth. What a blessing to have a God who came to earth in person to show us the qualities we should emulate.

Parents can learn Jesus characteristics by studying the Gospels (the first four chapters of the New Testament). Understanding what Jesus was like provides a pattern for parents to use when shaping their children's personality and character.

In Part II of this manual, I have listed for parents the character traits and qualities of Jesus I found in my reading of the New Testament. The idea is to provide a more concrete model that parents might use to rear children who emulate Jesus.

To tell you the truth, I have never heard of anyone listing Jesus' characteristics as a chart for parents to follow. I suspect it has been the topic in many Sunday School classes, but I never attended much Sunday School. If I haven't heard of such a thing, it may be that you haven't either. Parents can make their list, putting emphasis on those values that most need reinforcement and those that are most important to the family culture.

The beauty of this type of instruction is that it does not come packaged as commands with punishments. Knowing Jesus' attributes should allow a parent to better discern how Jesus would manage a situation. If we also silently pray for the Holy Spirit's assistance, it is very likely that our instruction will be current and consistent with God's will.

CHAPTER ONE

KEEPING THINGS IN PERSPECTIVE:

GOD COMES FIRST

It may seem strange that a child-rearing book would warn about "superlative" parenting. However, one of the early teachings of Jesus reminds us God should come before family: ***"Anyone who loves his father or mother more than me is not worthy of me; anyone who loves his son or daughter more than me is not worthy of me"*** (Matthew 10:37). This verse is consistent with the first four of the Ten Commandments that address the nature and the priority of our relationship to God (Jesus).

The Boy Scouts of America, founded in 1910, for over 100 years have had in their motto, "God, Country, Family." However, most Americans today no longer profess this priority in describing the optimum components of character. An internet search lead to the following article, which to me highlights that we are now in a post-Christian era, and how far our nation have become off track.

<u>Americans Don't Cite 'God, Family, Country' Quite Like The Cliché Goes</u>
By Cathy Lynn Grossman | Religion News Service
March 20, 2015

"'God, family and country' might make for a good country music tune, but that's not really how most Americans see the strongest influences on their personal identity.

The real order is family first (62%), followed by "being an American" (52%). 'Religious faith lolls way down in third place (38 %), if it's mentioned at all, according to a survey released March 19 by The Barna Group. The California-based Christian research company found another 18% of those surveyed said faith had a little to do with idea of who they are, and nearly 20% scored it at zero influence.

Barna surveyed 1,000 U.S. adults online from Feb. 3-11. 'Gen-Xers and Millennials have a reputation, for wanting to break away from traditional cultural narratives and to resist being 'boxed in' by what they perceive as limiting expectations,' Stone said."

Practicing child psychiatry confirmed for me that when parents put God first, child-rearing becomes much less complicated. Family-first parenting has its downside. Capable, loving parents who are highly invested in their children often head such families. On the surface such parenting is admirable. However, in these families, children may substitute the love and power of their parents for their God instead of Jesus. This provides a home atmosphere that does not encourage a child's Christian growth.

Human parents, because they are not God, are fallible. Children and parents feel safer and more secure when their faith assures them that a Heavenly Father is always available.

Problems occur when parents invest in their children to such a degree it that it becomes idolatry or child-worship. Parents may become ruled by what the child feels is satisfactory or entertaining. Disempowered parents lose their effectiveness. Such dynamics may have serious earthly and eternal-life consequences.

Parents' faith in a Heavenly Father provides a model of love and trust that children will emulate as their relationship with their parents develops. Earthly parents who put God first inform themselves of Biblical direction, causing them to be more confident and effective parents.

A God-first theology also diffuses the temptation of both parents and children to turn from God to worldliness. It is sad to see well-intended families charting their course without the benefit of the healthy God/family hierarchy described by the Ten Commandments and Jesus.

CHAPTER TWO

WHAT A FRIEND WE HAVE IN JESUS

God relates to us differently in the New Testament compared to the Old. God hasn't changed, but we have. Fifteen hundred years had passed since Moses received God's instructions for his human creatures. By the time Christ came to earth we humans should have learned and experienced the validity of God's rules and commandments. We should have become more civilized and receptive to a less threatening and more loving teaching approach. Throughout the New Testament Christ instructs us as if we are mature enough to understand the merit of his teachings and to apply them appropriately to our circumstances. Jesus refers to his disciples as "friends."

My first Christian parenting book, as I later became aware, had little information about parenting from the New Testament. Restudying the New Testament, after I had ten years of Christian maturity, revealed much that I previously missed. Christ left us with the Holy Spirit to expand upon His teaching, and I used Him as I reread the New Testament in preparation for this book. Christ's emphasis is on directing us to Heaven, but he assures us that living a life that qualifies us to join His heavenly family will more than cover us for having a better life on earth.

THE IMPORTANCE OF ORDER

A passion for order is a pervasive theme throughout the Bible. From creation being done on a schedule, through the celestial order of the universe and its physical laws, God's aversion to chaos is apparent. For me, the creation of order from chaos is a compelling argument of the existence of a Creator and shows us an important aspect of His nature.

It is interesting that Christ chose to come to earth during the time of the Roman Empire. Although Roman occupation of Israel during Christ's time was harsh, orderly protection provided by Roman force, "Pax Romanae" allowed Jesus and his disciples safe travel. Despite revulsion for slavery, Christ never proposed rebellion against the tyrannical government of Rome. He advised the Jews to pay their taxes saying, ***"Give unto Caesar what is Caesar's"*** (Matthew 22:21).

Though Jesus disapproved of the sterile, overly rigid, constricting way the Jewish religious leaders had interpreted God's law, His words and actions on earth did not encourage disorderliness or rebellion. He remained obedient to the laws that God commanded in the Old Testament; Jesus said in Matthew 5:17, ***"I came not to destroy the law but to fulfill it."***

There appears to be a modern political ramification to this lesson. Regardless of the abuse of power, anarchy is not a satisfactory substitute. Having an alternative structure to provide order should be in place before dismantling even a corrupt and sinful agency or government.

Children who grow up with healthy, loving, routine have personalities that reflect the security and stability of their home life. My work as a child psychiatrist brings me in contact with families where there is little order and routine. Some children live in homes that are chaotic, unpredictable and dangerous.

NOT A BOTTOM LINE GOD

It struck me as curious that, following Christ's numerous healing miracles described in the New Testament, there is no mention of what was later accomplished by the recipients. I was always looking for a report which says the crippled beggar went on to become the mayor of Jerusalem or maybe a famous preacher like Billy Graham. What was the end result of these miracles? What was the bottom-line? Jesus evidently did not see this as the crucial issue.

In I Corinthians 4: 2, the Apostle Paul says, "***Moreover it is required in stewards that a man be found faithful.***" He did not say, "It is required that a man be found successful." It would help if we parents had a similar attitude. Our culture stresses the bottom line. Parents judge their children's success by their grades, SAT scores, social status, how many and how exotic are the trips they are invited to go on with friends, how much playing time they get in a game, and other tangible bottom-line accomplishments. It would relieve a great burden for children if parents, like Christ, could adopt a more no-bottom-line approach. They would judge their children by what is in their hearts, what is their intent and how much and how sincere is their effort, not just by what they accomplished.

As this is God's pattern, it seems also likely He will judge parents by what they put into their children, rather than by what they get out of them. I frequently see parents who blame themselves for their children not meeting the bottom line of worldly expectations. A child has a natural tendency to grow up to be a mentally stable adult. That a child does not meet the worldly definition of having a successful childhood is sometimes good news. Working through difficulties in childhood can strengthen the child in becoming a successful adult. A child manifesting characteristics of Jesus rather than worldly ideals would be the best definition of a successful childhood. What do we know about this man/God Jesus?

CHAPTER THREE

WHO WAS JESUS?

Few people question that Jesus Christ was a man who once lived on earth. The disagreement comes about whether He was a teacher, a prophet or God. Old Testament prophets described Jesus' life 2000 to 500 years **before** His birth. They predicted that the Messiah would be born of a virgin in Bethlehem, enter Jerusalem in triumph on a donkey, be betrayed by His own people, remain silent before His accusers, die by crucifixion and be raised from the dead.

All these events happened, coming true almost two thousand years later, as recorded in the New Testament. I strongly recommend you check this out for yourself. For me, finding that these prophecies were fulfilled was an integral part of my becoming a believer.

The first four books of the Bible's New Testament, the Gospels, record Jesus' time on earth. The authors, Matthew, Mark, Luke, and John, wrote descriptions of Jesus' life and miracles, which were consistent with one another. The Bible states more than five hundred people reported they had seen the *resurrected* Jesus. These witnesses had nothing to gain from false testimony. To the contrary, after Jesus had been put to death, many Christians were tortured and killed for refusing to recant their claims of seeing Him alive. These martyrs would not have chosen death unless they had seen and experienced the truth of their conviction.

Jesus cannot solely be considered just a good teacher or prophet. He, Himself, said He was "God." Jesus would have to have been mad allowing himself to be crucified by pretending He was the Messiah. As a psychiatrist, I evaluate the mental status of patients and sometimes give expert testimony as to their sanity. I can attest that words and actions of Jesus that are described in the Bible do not suggest He was of unsound mind.

Christians believe the Holy Trinity consists of God the Father, Jesus the Son and the Holy Ghost. Jesus became God incarnate when he was conceived through a human mother, the Virgin Mary, and the Holy Spirit. He was born both fully human and fully God.

Supernatural events such as the Virgin birth, Jesus walking on water, or His resurrection can be studied, and their historical legitimacy judged; but it is foolish to try to measure them by today's scientific standards. Science judges truth using physical laws such as gravity, mass, acceleration and energy. God created these laws, but these laws do not govern the supernatural events of religion.

Taking a non-scientific approach does not require less intelligence or less critical reasoning and logic; it takes a different mindset. Deductions about the validity of events that occurred thousands of years ago must be made using the data that was available from the particular time period. The evidence, by its nature, will be circumstantial. It is illogical to withhold judgment because there is no direct evidence. Neither were there photographs, auditory recordings, physical remains or DNA proof to confirm Julius Caesar's life on earth, yet from ancient writings, we reason that he did exist.

In a court of law, circumstantial evidence can be adequate for a death sentence. It is sad that some refuse to accept the ample circumstantial evidence of Christ's existence, when it could result in eternal life.

Since Jesus walked the earth as a human, his Disciples were able to describe his actions and words. These are found in the first 140 pages of the New Testament. By reading the first 140 pages of the New Testament we can develop a clear picture of what Jesus was like.

CHAPTER FOUR

WHAT WAS JESUS LIKE?

Jesus is like God, The Father. God understood that there were no words that would adequately describe God, so He decided to show us. God was born of a human mother, so he was both man and God. When we know Jesus, we know God. John 14:9: ***"Jesus answered: Don't you know me, Philip, even after I have been among you such a long time? Anyone who has seen me has seen the Father. How can you say, 'Show us the Father'? Don't you believe that I am in the Father, and that the Father is in me?***

Parents who are teaching their children the principles of Jesus will also be building and strengthening their own Christian character. None of us can be a perfect guide for our children. Although we all are a work in process, parents are the conduit from which children will receive God's word. We are their best hope.

JESUS - NO RULES

In the New Testament, Jesus assumes that parents have integrated the Ten Commandments into their consciences, and that parents will continue to steep their children in these commandments until the children also have fully integrated them. Children are not born with a conscience already downloaded. God has given parents the responsibility for putting the data into the conscience. The data will be the attributes that Christ manifested while on earth. Jesus simplifies it for us. Jesus says the Ten Commandments, which God said parents should have ingrained on their children's heart, can be contained in only two commands: Matthew 22: 36-40. ***"Love the Lord with all your mind and heart and soul; the second is love your neighbor as yourself."***

Parents should be creative about how they put in the data. Maybe you should stick a list of Jesus' attributes on the refrigerator? The composition of the list and how it should be implemented could be discussed with a spouse and with the children. Look for times when children demonstrate Christ-like qualities, and put a star on the refrigerator list? How about for boys get a football helmet and put the stars on it. Make the list a regular topic in a family devotional? Maybe forming a small group of parents with similar age children to discuss and plan an approach might be helpful?

I started my list using the Fruit of the Spirit as described by the Apostle Paul.

THE FRUIT OF THE SPIRIT (Galatians 5:22-23)

"But the fruit of the Spirit is:
   Love
   Joy
   Peace
   Patience
   Kindness
   Goodness
   Faithfulness
   Gentleness
   Self Control

As behavior becomes more Christ-like, character blossoms forth and shows itself to others as the fruit of love, joy, peace, patience, kindness, goodness, faithfulness, gentleness and self control. By these fruit, or by their lack thereof, we can get some measure of our progress in becoming mature Christians

Simply consciously recognizing the "Fruit" as goals for our children should cause us to naturally encourage and reinforce them. Acknowledging approval when your child demonstrates Jesus' attributes will be more productive than correcting them when they do not show these qualities. Parents who exhibit the Fruit of the Spirit are a powerful template for their children's Christian growth. Although setting an example may be the best way to assist our children to develop these qualities, Jesus' attributes can be taught. Three of the fruit, Love, Patience and Self Control are of particular interest to a child psychiatrist.

LOVE

"Yes Jesus loves me, the Bible tells me so." As conveyed by this popular children's song, children enjoy a sweet acceptance of Jesus' love. Jesus was asked what was the most important commandments?" He replied: *"Love the Lord your God with all your heart and with all your soul and with all your mind. This is the first and greatest commandment."*

This Commandment from Christ underscores the great importance of parents putting God first as previously discussed. Parents need to look for opportunities to show their children examples of God's love. Bedtime prayers and grace before meals are a natural time to thank God and remind children of God's many blessings. Regular Church and Sunday school attendance can bring children under the influence of others who comfortably express their appreciation for God's love.

The second greatest commandment is recorded in Matthew 7:12, *"So in...everything, do to others what you would have them do to you."* Commonly known as The Golden Rule; it will lead children to develop empathy, a precursor of love for others.

When doing group therapy with adolescent patients, very few of them showed empathy for others in the group. Interestingly, improvement in their psychiatric problem often coincided with their ability to become empathetic. Children who exhibit empathy tend to be liked and respected. One way to put into practice this commandment is for your child to observe and to help as you serve others. Serving others is a Christ-like example of love. It fosters generous, kind and good children.

When trying to love your neighbor I found this mnemonic from minster and author Charles Swindoll helpful:
Listen
Overlook
Value
Express

God's love for each of us should be very comforting; ***"If God is for us, who can be against us?"*** Romans 8:31. Parental love seems the closest a human comes to approximating the love of God, our Heavenly Father. The opposite, child abuse and neglect, reflects the essence of ungodliness and sin.

Being a loving parent thankfully should not require the suffering Jesus underwent for our benefit, but it will always include personal sacrifice. Parents with Christ-like love will make child-rearing decisions with their children's best interest at heart, even if it requires sacrifice. Love overrides most errors in parental management. How fortunate are children when loving parents direct their lives? How blessed we are to have such a loving God?

PATIENCE

Jesus was a very patient person. When He was only twelve years old, his parents lost Him for three days. They found him discussing Scripture with scholarly Rabbis. Luke 2: 46-47. ***"After three days they found him in the temple courts, sitting among the teachers, listening to them and asking them questions. Everyone who heard him was amazed at his understanding and answers."*** Jesus was a child prodigy, yet he waited until he was thirty years old to start his ministry.

Although He knew He had only four years to complete His work on earth; He never appeared to have been in a hurry. He always had time to talk with children and people in need. He took time from his busy schedule for meditation and prayer. The "get it now" generation is contrary to the way of Christ.

Relief from effort, frustration and discomfort has always driven human behavior. However, today's technology and affluence have enabled us to reach a level where many of our creature comforts have been achieved. Many Americans now consider access to entertainment and freedom from boredom a "right."

A media that provides instant satisfaction and increasing exhilaration encourages the entitled attitude of parents and children. Today, a child's value system sometimes can be shaped more by the media and peers than by parents.

Parents, not having the benchmark of Biblical instruction, may judge their effectiveness by whether the child seems to approve of the parents' methods. This allows children to manipulate and control their parents. As a result, immature, confused children find themselves setting their own moral compass.

Rick Warren's book, The Purpose Driven Life, underscores life on earth is not an end unto itself. He reminds us we are short-time visitors on earth, as we prepare for our real purpose, living our eternal life in Heaven.

Parenting has a close analogy. Children are merely passing through their relatively short childhood in the process of developing into competent, discerning, stable adults. Childhood is not an end unto itself. It is counterproductive when parents put too much emphasis on providing their children "successful" childhoods.

My experience as a child psychiatrist supports the value of children being taught to be patient. Parents who encourage their children's quest for immediate gratification are doing them a disservice. It is risky to assist children in "growing up too fast."

Parents, who encourage their young daughters to dress and behave older, may push them into relationship with older boys and temptations they do not have the maturity to handle. For some teenagers, romance can be perilous. Parents and children may pay a high price when they elevate a teenage crush to the importance of mature intimacy.

I have seen parents allow their child to talk all night on the phone with a boyfriend or girlfriend so they can "work things out." Parents may allow the child-couple to spend hours in the bedroom with the door closed because the parents "don't want to intrude on their privacy." Parents will not take family trips without including their child's boyfriend or girlfriend.

Parents seldom appreciate how dangerous hurrying up their child's development can be. Teen-couples may come to feel their entire life revolves around one another. They become desperate when their out-of-perspective romance falls apart. I have interviewed several outstanding young people who have committed, or come close to committing, violent acts because of immature jealousy.

Childhood and teenage years are a time for developing strengths that will be used when children leave home to make a separate life. This should not be rushed. Over-emphasis on providing your child a successful childhood, particularly if based on cultural views about what is "cool," can be shortsighted and dangerous.

SELF CONTROL

Can you imagine the degree of self-control required for a powerful Almighty God to come from Heaven to earth and submit Himself, without resistance, to the pain and injustice of this world?

Consider the self-control and self sacrifice required to allow yourself to be taken prisoner without using your God-powers. In Matthew 26:50-54, Jesus said to Peter, ***'Put your sword back in its place,' Jesus said to him, for all who draw*** *the sword will die by the sword. Do you think I cannot call on my Father, and he will at once put at my disposal more than twelve legions of angels?"*

How did He resist using his supernatural power to avoid crucifixion? Before becoming a Christian, stories of Christ's passive acceptance of insult, persecution, and death were troubling to me. I viewed his passivity as "weakness," very contrary to what I expected in my God. What a difference 10 years, Bible study, and the Holy Spirit makes. Christ's never-wavering determination to sacrifice Himself for our salvation has become my model for courage.

Expecting children to exhibit characteristics of Christ is an example of the higher standard set in the New Testament. It addresses our children's heart and attitudes, not just their behaviors.

ATTITUDE

Although I found nothing in the Gospels describing Christ's "attitude," there are multiple references in the New Testament of Christ knowing what people are thinking and feeling. Christ's references to "what is in a man's heart" could be construed as "attitude." John MacArthur, in his book entitled What the Bible Says About Parenting, says the Fifth Commandment, "Honor your mother and father," is as much about "attitude" as it is about "obedience."

He says obedience without honor is nothing more than hypocrisy, and, if there is honor, obedience follows easily. Parents sometimes ignore a child's bad attitude and are satisfied if the child just minds. Suppose a child grudgingly does a chore while demonstrating a disrespectful attitude. From my experience, the lack of honor is a more serious problem. Parents are better off dealing with this problem sooner than later. It is a lot less difficult to correct a grumbling 8 year old who kicks the door when told to clean up his/her room, than a 16 year old who curses and drives off in the family car.

REV. CHARLES SWINDOL ON ATTITUDE:

"The longer I live, the more I realize the impact of attitude on life.

Attitude, to me, is more important than facts. It is more important than the past, than education, than money, than circumstances, than failures, than successes, than what other people think or say or do. It is more important than appearance, . . . giftedness or skill. It will make or break a company . . a church . . . a home.

The remarkable thing is, we have a choice every day regarding the attitude we will embrace for that day. We cannot change our past . . . we cannot change the fact that people will act in a certain way. We cannot change the inevitable. The only thing we can do is play on the one string we have, and that is our attitude . . . . I am . . . convinced that life is 10% what happens to me and 90% how I react to it.

And so it is with you . . . we are in charge of our attitudes."

You can't go wrong with starting your list of Christ's characteristics to emulate than with the Apostle Paul's "Fruit of the Spirit." In addition to the Fruit of the Spirit, there are many other characteristics of Christ in the New Testament to be discovered and model. The following are the ones that came to my attention. Feel free to add some from my list to yours. Then be amazed at what the Holy Spirit points out to you when you search the New Testament for yourself.

CHAPTER FIVE

DAN'S LIST OF OTHER CHARACTERISTICS OF CHRIST

COMPASSIONATE - OLD TESTAMENT

The Old Testament has many references to God's compassion. Examples include:

> Exodus 33:19 - *And the Lord said, "I will cause all my goodness to pass in front of you, and I will proclaim my name, the Lord, in your presence. I will have mercy on whom I will have mercy, and I will have compassion on whom I will have compassion."*
> Nehemiah 9:17 - *"They refused to listen and failed to remember the miracles you performed among them. They became stiff-necked and in their rebellion appointed a leader in order to return to their slavery. But you are a forgiving God, gracious and compassionate, slow to anger and abounding in love. Therefore you did not desert them,"*
> Psalms 116:5 - *"The Lord is gracious and righteous; our God is full of compassion."*

COMPASSIONATE - NEW TESTAMENT

Our understanding of the Holy Trinity assures us that Jesus is God. We expect in the New Testament that Christ will be compassionate. This is certainly the case. However, Christ's compassion shown in the New Testament has a different quality. It has a tenderness that is not as apparent in the Old Testament in the way God is described. Christ's concerns seem more "human."

Consider Jesus' reaction as He heard of his friend, Lazarus,' death: *"Where have you laid him?" he asked. "Come and see, Lord," they replied. Jesus wept. Then the Jews said. See how he loved him!"* (John 11:34-36, 34)

In Luke 19:41-42, "As he approached Jerusalem and saw the city, he wept over it and said, 'If you, even you, had only known on this day what would bring you peace—but now it is hidden from your eyes.'"

Compassion in the New Testament seems more individual and personal. In the parable of the prodigal son (Luke 15:20), Jesus said, *"So he got up and went to his father. But while he was still a long way off, his father saw him and was filled with compassion for him; he ran to his son, threw his arms around him and kissed him."*

Jesus identifies even with our relatively minor human needs, such as the discomfort of missing meals. Matthew 15:32, *"Jesus called his disciples to him and said, "I have compassion for these people; they have already been with me three days and have nothing to eat. I do not want to send them away hungry, or they may collapse on the way."*

Joseph, Jesus' stepfather, is not mentioned in the Bible after he and Mary took Jesus to Jerusalem for Passover when Jesus was 12 years old (Luke 2:41.) There is speculation that Mary was widowed some time after that trip. Jesus, being the oldest son, would have assumed financial responsibility for the family. Notice Jesus' immediate, compassionate response to the widow who has lost her only son (Luke 7:12-15), *"As he approached the town gate, a dead person was being carried out - the only son of his mother, and she was a widow. And a large crowd from the town was with her. When the Lord saw her, his heart went out to her and he said, "Don't cry." Then he went up and touched the bier they were carrying him on, and the bearers stood still. He said, "Young man, I say to you, get up! The dead man sat up and began to talk, and Jesus gave him back to his mother."* It comforts me greatly that Jesus, my intermediary on judgement day, will be so in tune with our humanness and have compassion.

HUMILITY RATHER THAN PRIDE

One of the most extraordinary characteristics of Jesus, the Son of God, was His humility. Can you imagine a God who would choose to become incarnate by being born in a manger to a poor carpenter and his wife? He chose to be unremarkable in His physical appearance or countenance. He had no formal education and never traveled more than 60 miles from where He was born. He never married or had children. He ministered to the poor and needy, while He was dependent on others for money and food. He was arrested, ridiculed, spit upon, beaten, forced to wear a crown of thorns and carry His own cross through Jerusalem. He allowed himself to be crucified below a sign saying *"This is the King of the Jews"* (John 19:19).

If God didn't feel humility was essential, surely He would have written a different script for His Son's life. If we are to be like Jesus, humility, not pride, needs to be the cornerstone of our lives. Christ said (Matthew 18:4), *"Therefore, whoever humbles himself like this child is the greatest in the kingdom of heaven."* Matthew 23:12, **"For whoever exalts himself will be *humbled, and whoever humbles himself will be exalted."*.**

If parents want their children to manifest humility, the best way to do this is for the parents to exhibit this quality. This will require a change in direction for many for us. Having been reared by parents, particularly fathers and coaches, who emphasize "pride" as the greater virtue, encouraging "humility" requires a mind-set that runs counter-culture. Part of the problem may be semantics. Our culture seems to use the word "pride" as a synonym for courage, perseverance and determination. The "pride" referred to in the Bible sounds more like self-righteousness, self- exultation and conceit. This type of pride is more similar to the self-promoting showboating so commonly performed by professional athletes. Humility doesn't taunt opponents or trash talk. Such behaviors clearly are renounced in both the Old and the New Testament.

Parents may be encouraging these behaviors in their children by buying jerseys and other paraphernalia glamorizing these prideful celebrities. On the other hand, when celebrities who demonstrate concern for others, humility, self-control, moderation, tolerance, respect and the importance of their faith are identified, parents can affirm these. Teaching children about Christ's humility through Bible study will emphasize the importance God gives to humility. Praising your children when they show acts of humility, service and kindness teach children their parents also value humility. We know that God wants us to be humble. From my experience, it is the humble, not the proud, who I most appreciate, respect and admire.

OBEDIENCE

Jesus Christ was obedient to His father. He gave up his Godly power and suffered a humiliating and painful death so that His father's *"will be done"* (Matthew 26:42). Obedience to authority sometimes seems to be a loss of personal independence and freedom. God's commandments and rules for living can seem binding and restrictive. However, the Bible says by becoming *"slaves"* to God, we actually become *"free."* (Romans 6:17)

John Newton, the Anglican priest and former English slave ship captain who wrote the hymn "Amazing Grace," also wrote a poem called the "The Kite and Its String," which shows how loss of restraint can bring failure and disappointment, not freedom.

"The Kite and It's String"
by John Newton (edited by shortening)

Once upon a time a paper kite

Was mounted to a wondrous height,
"Were I but free, I'd take a flight,
And pierce the clouds beyond their sight, But, ah! like a poor pris'ner bound, My string confines me near the ground;
It tugged and pulled, while thus it spoke, To break the string - at last it broke.
Deprived at once of all its stay, In vain it tried to soar away; Unable its own weight to bear,
It fluttered downward through the air; Unable its own course to guide,
The winds soon plunged it in the tide.
Ah! foolish kite, thou hadst no wing, How could'st thou fly without a string!
My heart replied, "O Lord, I see How much this kite resembles me!"

There are analogies of this in child rearing. Adolescents who abide by their parents rules find they are given much more freedom than when they are resisting or breaking them. For children, obedience usually begins with a fear of the power of the parent. A child will not learn rules from someone seen as powerless. Obedience makes it possible for children to conduct themselves in ways that permits them to safely relate to others. Failure to teach these lessons result in children having to learn rules from a less sympathetic and sometimes dangerous outside world. They are like the kite with the string broken. Loving parents rear obedient children to protect them from danger, until the children have the maturity to understand, appreciate and internalize their parents' values.

Children are protected by their obedience to God's Commandments until their faith has matured to the level that they follow the law, because they emulate Christ. Neither God's nor parents' unconditional love imply there are no consequences for bad behavior. Unconditional love has to do with a parent's, and God's, forgiving nature and abiding love.

Control and discipline of children are important features of this love. Does the child see discipline as loving? Usually not. However, when the parents' acts of control and discipline are done with love, acting in the best interest of their children, the children sense this. The parents' love overrides the child's temporary anger and sense of unfairness. This emotion is similar to the way human Christian adults may feel about situations they initially assume were unloving acts by a punitive or neglectful God. Their faith in God's love sustains them until they understand or can accept God's will. Likewise, children later will understand their parents' "restrictive rules" were loving and beneficial.

SUFFERING

Christ suffered greatly on earth. Does emulating Christ include suffering? The Bible does not promote suffering for its own sake. It is the suffering that comes from sacrificing to serve Christ and others that is valued. Living a Godly life can lead to persecution from a worldly culture that may feel threatened by Christian values, ***"For it is commendable if a man bears up under the pain of unjust suffering because he is conscious of God"*** (1Peter 2:19).

I had never thought of suffering as an opportunity. Most of my lifetime I have been trying to avoid it. That a loving God would allow or seems indifferent to our suffering has been hard for me to understand. One explanation is God created man with the freedom to choose between right and wrong. Designing a world with only good choices would not have permitted free will; the option of making a bad choice must also be available. Another reason could be that suffering and hopelessness are circumstances which may cause humans to turn to God. There is no way for us to know God's reasoning until we enter Heaven.

Children may feel their parents are being mean and unfair, even though the parents are acting in their children's best interest. Parents use their knowledge and past experience to make fairly accurate assumptions about future consequences to their children. God has knowledge of the entire history of the human race and the ability to know the future. When children grow up, they look back at their parents' actions, to which they originally objected, as being beneficial. I remember situations in my life that, at the time, seemed unfortunate or unfair, where I am now grateful to God for working out things the way He did.

    If we experience our children incorrectly labeling our parenting methods, which are loving and in their best interest, as unfair, why do we adult humans so harshly judge our Heavenly Father? Fortunately, God does not seem to be swayed by whether we understand or approve of how He shapes our lives. Parents sometimes compromise doing what is right for their children because they too much want the children to understand and appreciate their methods. This isn't the way God does it, and it does not work well for human child rearing.

    Thankfully, parents are very invested in keeping their children safe. When children or young people die, it tests our faith. It is tempting to blame God for not protecting them. Why would a loving God permit this to happen? Before we are too hard on God, we might consider how we human parents approach keeping our children from harm.

    Good parents make countless decisions which potentially expose their children to danger or even death. When parents encourage children to walk, they expose them to later risks, such as running in front of a car. When they allow their children to play with other children, they increase the possibility they could develop a life-threatening disease. Parents would never let their children go near water if they wanted to completely protect them from drowning. No sports would be permitted because of possible injury. They would never, never allow their children to drive a car.

Parents have good reasons for exposing their children to these risks. They realize children will never achieve their potential if they protect them from all risk.

In 2006, I made a trip to Romania to consult with Livada, a Christian organization dedicated to moving orphans from government institutions into Christian group homes. The previous communist regime had placed thousands of children into institutions and provided them with what they felt was the safest environment. Infants were protected from harm by being restrained in their beds by sterile sheets. There was minimal contact with other humans, protecting the children from the risk of harmful bacteria. As a result of this misguided care, the children became retarded intellectually and interpersonally. Even their physical health was subpar. If you can imagine such a thing, the government decided to treat some infants' developmental delays and poor health by providing them with periodic blood transfusions, resulting in some becoming infected with AIDs.

If parents reared their children free of risk, it would cause the children to be intellectually, interpersonally and physically stunted. Loving, effective parents do expose their children to life situations that can have dangerous consequences. Parents must judge if the benefit merits the risk. The parents' goal is to get their children through childhood "alive" but with the skills and potential of a competent adult.

Jesus' goal for us is to begin living the goodness on earth that we will manifest in Heaven. His emphasis seems to be to prepare us for Heaven, not necessarily to avoid worldly death. God's rationale for allowing us to experience life, with its many dangers and risks, makes sense to me when I consider that parents have the ability to protect their children from almost all risk, yet they decide not to do this. Why should God's decision to take a similar approach seem unfair? God could have created us to be like robots, and we would have been a lot safer. God could have us pass through life on earth without risk. However, to do this would take away free choice and keep us from our potential. *"We know that suffering creates endurance, endurance creates character, and character creates confidence"* (Romans 5:4).

FORGIVING

Christ commanded that we be forgiving, and forgiveness was an essential aspect of His character. *"Bear with each other and forgive whatever grievances you may have against one another. Forgive as the Lord forgave you."* (Colossians 3:13). *"And when you stand praying, if you hold anything against anyone, forgive them, so that your Father in heaven may forgive you your sins"* (Mark 11:26). *"Be kind and compassionate to one another, forgiving each other, just as in Christ God forgave you."* (Ephesians 4:32). As Jesus was being crucified, He prayed for his murderers (Luke 23:34): Then said Jesus, *"Father, forgive them; for they know not what they do."*). If our children and we are to be like Christ, we will have to be forgiving.

There is a worldly reason to forgive others. Internalized hostility and anger is a precursor to depression and destructive behavior toward others and oneself. People who are able to let go of their anger and forgive a perpetrator usually sense a wave of relief. It frees them to have more energy to invest in satisfying and productive activities. They are happier and more content.

The Apostle Paul said, *"In your anger do not sin: Do not let the sun go down while you are still angry, and do not give the devil a foothold."* (Ephesians 4:26-27).

SERVING OTHERS

"Who, being in very nature God, did not consider equality with God something to be grasped, but made himself nothing, taking the very nature of a servant, being made in human likeness" (Philippians 2:6-7). *"For even the Son of*

Man did not come to be served, but to serve, and to give his life as a ransom for many" (Mark 10:45).

You probably know people who are committed to serving others. Such people are described as kind and good. Kindness and goodness are listed as Fruit of the Spirit by Paul in *Galatians 5:22*. There are other places in the Bible where we are directed to be kind and good: *"Each of us should please his neighbor for his good, to build him up"* (Rom 15:2).

Some time ago, I made a self-assessment of how I was progressing on my Christian journey. Comparing myself to the characteristics of Christ, of course revealed many deficiencies. The most apparent to me was in the area of serving others. That's a big one! I am working on correcting it.

Serving others is the soil for growing the Fruit of the Spirit. When we model and teach our children to serve others, they are put in a mode where they will be showing love, joy, patience, peace, kindness, goodness, faithfulness, gentleness and self- control.

An excellent opportunity for addressing this is when children complain of being "bored." Doing something to help others should remedy their bored condition, and, at the same time, improve their mood and attitude. A heart for serving others should be immune to boredom.

MORAL

Jesus was perfectly moral despite being tempted like humans on earth. Nothing in the New Testament suggested Jesus ever sinned; *"For we do not have a high priest who is unable to sympathize with our weaknesses, but we have one who has been tempted in every way, just as we are - yet was without sin."* (Hebrews 4:15).

KNOWLEDGABLE ABOUT SCRIPTURE

Jesus often quoted Old Testament Scripture. We should do likewise.

ACCEPTING

Jesus was criticized for his association with "society misfits." For example, while Jesus was having dinner at Matthew's house, many tax collectors and "sinners" came and ate with him and his disciples. *"When the Pharisees saw this, they asked his disciples, "Why does your teacher eat with tax collectors and ' sinners'?"* On hearing this, Jesus said, *"It is not the healthy who need a doctor, but the sick. For I have not come to call the righteous, but sinners"* (Matthew 9:11-13).

TAUGHT BY EXAMPLE

Jesus' actions were consistent with his words.

PRAYERFUL

Parent/God prayer has similarities to child/parent communication. Parents want their children to communicate with them. It assures parents that their children respect and trust them. Their communication shows the parents how well the children are accepting the parents' teaching and values. It is disheartening to parents if children only communicate with them when they want something. God must surely feel the same way about our begging prayers. Particularly, when He knows granting a request is not in our best interest. I suspect God prefers it when we "talk to Him." Jesus spent the night before his crucifixion in prayer. Praying is an important quality of Jesus that needs to be taught.

God answering prayer strengthens our faith, but we often have a misconception about how this happens.

CHAPTER SIX

A CHRISTIAN MISCONCEPTION

FINDING UNDERSTANDING IN PRISON

In 2018-2019 I volunteered to teach a sixteen month theology course to 34 servant prisoner leaders incarcerated at the Hutchins Texas State prison on its Faith Based Unit. My motivation for going to prison was to better my self evaluation that showed I was deficient in Christ's emphasis on "service." The prison's motivation for using me was the thought that my training as a psychiatrist, as well as being a committed Christian, might add a useful dimension to the prisoner's study. The course I taught was primarily a review of what these men had learned from required classes taught by ministers and lay church leaders during the prisoners' up to two year stay.

Teaching prisoners was a positive influence on my own understanding and faith. I concluded that except for life circumstances and God's grace, many of us could have been in prison and they out.

The question that first came to my mind was, Why is the recidivism for prisoners so high? Many of the prisoners had four or more separate stays in prison.

In our discussion group we decided the reason they kept returning to prison was a misconception about how Christianity can protect them. Like many things I learned from prisoners, the misconception also applied to many of us on the outside. The misconception is that being a Christian equips us with a tool kit of special knowledge that, when applied, will allow us to avoid life's traumas - or to at least be able to fix them when they occur. If a crisis occurs, we expect Christianity to be our "get our of jail free card" When we get into trouble, we may pray and look to the Bible. In between these pitfalls, we may feel little incentive to live immersed in a Christian life style.

The prisoners took considerable solace in Paul's words as recorded in Ephesians 6:18, ***"Therefore put on the full armor of God, so that when the day of evil comes, you may be able to stand your ground, and after you have done everything, to stand firm then, with the belt of truth buckled around your waist, with the breastplate of righteousness in place, and with your feet fitted with the readiness that comes from the gospel of peace. In addition to all this, take up the shield of faith, with which you can extinguish all the flaming arrows of the evil one. Take the helmet of salvation and the sword of the Spirit, which is the word of God.***

However, they didn't notice that Paul says to put on armor **before** evil comes. It is the Christian life we are living that is our armor, not something that is to be strapped on during a crisis. We don't realize that the way we are living our every day lives is the armor that protects us. Our vulnerability begins when we slack on little things that we can do, like daily prayer, Bible reading, Bible study group, attending church regularly, going to Sunday School and keeping our thoughts from becoming darker.

Teaching prisoners and our children to practice Jesus' attributes focuses on what they need to be doing rather than what they should not be doing. In the process, children and their family become immersed in a life style that keeps them in protective armor long before troubles occur. Having a list of Christ-like qualities will remind us to encourage them when children show them.

Parents looking for Christ's qualities to praise in their children should make childhood a more positive experience. The alternative, parents being over vigilant to stop bad behavior, is a negative approach and can make childhood unhappy for parents and children.

As children mature, their conscience will remind them to avoid sinful behavior. Sin has a way of working out its own punishment, and children and adults will naturally come to see this.

Conversion includes being born again with the possibility of becoming a new and improved person. This is not automatic. Living a Christian life is more involved than just being converted.

The Apostle Paul was familiar with this problem. Romans 6:19 **"I am using an example from everyday life because of your human limitations. Just as you used to offer yourselves as slaves to impurity and to ever-increasing wickedness, so now offer yourselves as slaves to righteousness leading to holiness."** To just stop having bad habits is not enough. Fill that time with good activity or you will stay susceptible to wrongdoing.

The directions for aiming at Heaven are found in the Bible, and they are doable. Accept the challenge of living a Christian life. It is simple and within anyone's grasp. When living God's way becomes a routine, problems seem to take care of themselves.

Here is an example I used with the prisoners. Suppose you are at a friend's birthday party being held at a bar. You say "no thanks" to a beer he offers, and you congratulate your "born-again-self" on how you have resisted another temptation. Actually this is an example of the common misconception of how the armor of Christianity can protect you.

A more positive scenario would be that your friend did not even invite you to his party because he has come to recognize that you are "not as much fun when you don't drink," or, even if you had been invited, you couldn't have gone because your Bible Study group met that night. Which man in both scenarios would be the most likely to stay out of prison?

Many of us outside share the same misconception as the prisoners. We tend to see Christianity as something we can use when troubles brew rather than a way to live our lives. Helping your children manifest characteristics of Christ will remind you also to recognize and strengthen you own Christ-like traits.

Bible Study, praying, reading the Bible, living in a wholesome family, being with Christian friends and doing kind things for others will be an example that your children will emulate. The New Testament is filled with advice about how you can be a good person. The ultimate example of a good person is Jesus Christ.

The list I made in the previous chapter is not the Gospel. Reading the New Testament and finding Jesus' characteristics for yourself is strongly encouraged. Add what you discover in the Bible to my list. Be intentional about making Jesus' qualities a part of your child's personality. Circle those which you feel are most important or those that need the most reinforcement. Check off the ones that have been accomplished.

Even thoughts need to considered:

Proverbs 23:7 ***"As someone thinks within himself, so he is."***

Romans 12:2 ***"Do not copy the behavior and customs of this world, but let God transform you into a new person by changing the way you think. Then you will learn to know God's will for you, which is good and pleasing and perfect."***

Philippians 4:8 ***"Whatever is noble, whatever is right, whatever is pure, whatever is lovely, whatever is admirable - if anything is excellent or praiseworthy - think about such things."***

Mahatma Gandhi said:
"Your beliefs become your thoughts,
Your thoughts become your words,
Your words become your actions,
Your actions become your habits,
Your habits become your values,
Your values become your destiny."

Jesus said in John 18:36, ***"My kingdom is not of this world. But now my kingdom is from another place."*** Christian doctrine primarily directs us to be eligible for the Kingdom of Heaven - God's Kingdom. This is something that is much better and more lasting than just achieving a successful worldly existence. Fortunately, reaching for Heaven can lead to a more successful worldly life.

C.S. Lewis in, <u>The Joyful Christian</u> said "Aim at Heaven and you will get Earth 'thrown in': aim at Earth and you will get neither."

Sam Walton, the founder of Walmart, built his business on Christian principles. He is an excellent example how reaching for Heaven can also bring rewards on earth.

My friend, Foster Poole, the founder of the successful Dallas Sample House gift stores, had a similar Christian application for work:

Rules For Building A Business
Foster and Nancy Poole

- Include God and the church in your life.
- Love and enjoy your family.
- Spend time with friends and make meaningful relationships.
- Help people in any way you can.
- Laugh, especially at yourself. If you can't laugh at yourself, you're in trouble.
- Treat everyone with respect, and let them know that they are important. to you.
- Have a happy atmosphere. Smile and set the example.
- Money doesn't buy happiness. Love people and not things.

- Don't wait to do something until everything is perfect. That day will never come.
- Stay busy, It helps keep you young.
- Enjoy every day. You can't get it back.

Unfortunately, doing everything recommended in this manual is no guarantee that everything will go smoothly. What if you are at an impasse? Have you thought your child might need to see a psychiatrist?

CHAPTER SEVEN

WHEN YOUR CHILD NEEDS A PSYCHIATRIST?

Being a Christian is a big help but does not guarantee that children will be immune from problems growing up. Modern discoveries about human development and behavior can help in understanding a child and can provide guidance or treatment when parenting reaches an impasse. For example, counseling for parents in marital turmoil may prevent a divorce. Recognizing a child's learning disability and providing remedial teaching and schooling can expand his or her educational potential. The diagnosis and successful treatment of attention deficit disorder, depression, drug abuse, obsessive compulsive disorder, and other disorders during childhood not only results in better adjusted children, but treatment may also prevent mental illness when they become adults. Suicidal adolescents and children can be identified, protected, and successfully treated. Out-of-control children and teenagers may be hospitalized to interrupt dangerous, self-destructive behavior.

Sometimes a child may come with biologic mental and/or emotional limitations that may require skills that can be beyond what the parents can provide in the home setting. Medication may make it possible for a child to be managed at home by parents rather in a boarding school or in residential treatment.

When psychiatric theories and treatment are supported by Scripture, it increases our confidence in applying them. This does not mean medical treatments not found in the Bible are suspect or invalid. The Bible does not mention insulin, antibiotics, or chemotherapy, yet we use them feeling no conflict with Biblical teaching. A reasonable perspective is for parents to be cautious about accepting an explanation, recommendation, or treatment for their child if it contradicts Biblical teaching.

Learning and practicing Christian principles taught in the Bible can show the way for becoming a righteous person and an effective parent. It sounds easy and it usually it is. Why does it not always work?

Sometimes God has something else in mind. There is no way we can know or understand God's providence. Parents may blame themselves because their children have problems. Parents need to remind themselves of the loving effort they put into their children when the children were younger. Children with disabilities need buffering from a sometimes harsh and insensitive environment. If the parents had not intervened, the child would have never accomplished the developmental level he/she had reached. However, there comes a time when parents' protection must be lessened. A therapist who evaluates the family at this stage may inaccurately conclude that the parents' protection of the child is the problem itself. Parents should be reassured it is not their fault. What they put into their child should be recognized. If parents understood God will judge them by what they "put in" to their children rather than what they "get out" of them, it would relieve a lot of pressure for both parents and children.

God imposes no bottom line to child rearing. What is important is that we can be confident we have reared our children with love, and that we have conscientiously tried to fulfill God's parenting direction as described in the Bible.

Some parents have great difficulty in asking for professional help for their child, even if it seems necessary. They may fear that their child will be put on unneeded medication. A better understanding of how the brain works might be helpful.

BRAIN FUNCTION (Overview)

There are billions of nerve cells in the brain, most interconnect with the others. Electric impulses go from one nerve to another across a microscopic space called a synapse. Chemical substances named neurotransmitters are present in the synapse. The medications used for psychiatric disorders alter the quantity of neurotransmitters in the synapses. This alters the electrical flow, which will then effect the way a person thinks, feels and/or reacts.

Some medications have partial selectivity for specific areas of the brain. For example, stimulants seem to have the greatest effect in the area of the brain controlling motor activity and attention span. Psychoactive medication offers the possibility of altering this biology. The medicines used to treat Attention Deficit Disorder (ADD) have proved to be remarkably beneficial. Most have the advantage that they are effective within an hour or two after being administered. There is very little down side for a "trial" of ADD medications. Often the decision to stop or continue a medicine can be made after one dose. However, medication alone seldom is a "cure."

There has been tremendous progress in the development of effective and safe psychoactive medications for children. Although children are sometimes prescribed unneeded medication, it is more common for children who need medication not to receive it. There are many misconceptions and/or myths about the use of psychoactive medications.

CHAPTER EIGHT

MYTHS ABOUT PSYCHOACTIVE MEDICATIONS

QUESTIONS THAT MAY KEEP PARENTS FROM SEEKING HELP

Couldn't giving a child medication interfere with character formation? Isn't it better for the child to learn to overcome and cope with a weakness?

> Answer: Yes. Coping is better. However, from my experience, the reason most parents seek professional help is that it has become clear that the child does not have sufficient interpersonal skill, general knowledge, self control or control over his life circumstances to develop these coping skills. Treatment should help them to cope sufficiently, so that the child can more positively use character-building life experiences. Parents should avoid responding to every bad behavior with, Have you taken your medicine today? This erodes the child efforts at self-control.

Will my child have to be on medication for the rest of his/her life?

> Answer: Very rarely. It is unusual that a child will require medication into adulthood. More often, the doctor will discontinue the medication if it appears the child is back on track or if the medication is not clearly effective or needed. Keep in mind that you can stop medicine anytime your are not comfortable with your child taking it. Doctors can't make a parent do anything. They can only prescribe. The parents will decide whether to fill the prescription or give it.

Should I get several opinions to assure we have the correct diagnosis?

Answer: Most doctors are comfortable with their patients getting other opinions. However, in child psychiatry, this sometimes results in frustrating and confusing "doctor shopping." It is a mistake to keep seeing different doctors with the expectation that the problem would be solved if you find the correct diagnosis. An accurate diagnosis is important for guiding the treatment approach. However, in child psychology, except for Attention Deficit Disorder, science has not yet established that there is a specific medicine type that is effective for a specific psychiatric diagnosis. The same medications may be used for multiple diagnosis. Going to a doctor who makes a more accurate diagnosis does not necessarily mean that the treatment will be changed. Because a child is going through changing developmental stages, hormones and family dynamics, it is complicated. I suggest you find a doctor of good reputation and of good training with whom you are comfortable. If you are not satisfied with the result, I would get another opinion about the treatment, but not because getting a different diagnosis will result in a new medication that will be specific for the new diagnosis.

Will medication "cover up" an underlying psychological conflict rather than allow it to be treated?

Answer: Children more commonly develop symptoms because of a biological deficit (attention disorder, bipolar disorder, learning disorder), rather than because of unconscious intra-psychic conflict. However, how the child adjusts to the deficit is highly related to how his significant figures (parents, teachers, sibs, friends), interact with him/her.

People often say psychiatric disorders are caused by "chemical imbalance." Can't blood tests determine the diagnosis?

Answer: Not yet. Research is being done in this area. However, it is common for the doctor to order blood tests. These are usually to rule out some physical cause for the problems such as lead poisoning, thyroid disease and to have a baseline for the normal blood measurements. During the course of treatment, blood tests may be done to monitor the blood level of a medication or to assure that the child is actually swallowing the medicine and not spitting it out. Also, periodic blood tests can confirm that the baseline blood tests have not changed, indicating a side effect.

COMMON MISCONCEPTIONS

Children with ADD never function as well as non ADD children.

Answer: To the contrary, ADD children may have an increased ability to focus in certain situations (when doing something they enjoy or when under unusual pressure).

Learning Disabilities are helped by psychoactive medications.

Answer: Not usually. Medication is most likely to be prescribed for a learning disabled child because there is an additional diagnosis (ADD, depression, obsessive compulsive disorder, bipolar disorder, anxiety disorder, etc.). Learning disabilities such as dyslexia, dysgraphia, dyscalulia require special teaching and tutoring and are not usually helped by medication.

Can adult psychiatric disorders be predicted from childhood problems?

Answer: not usually. Although the roots of many adult disorders can be seen in adolescence or childhood, symptoms usually are not specific enough to predict a definite diagnosis. Symptoms of temper outbursts, aggressiveness, withdrawal, and/or lack of attentiveness may, later in life, subside. Time and response to treatment usually clarify the if there is there will be an adult psychiatric diagnosis.

Besides for ADD, What medications are commonly prescribed?

Answer: Information about specific psychoactive medications used in childhood should be discussed with your physician or pharmacist.

CHAPTER NINE

SENDING YOUR CHILD TO COLLEGE

Nowhere in the Bible does it say there are stages of our lives that are exempt from God's law. Somehow we have gotten the mistaken idea that colleges are free from God's scrutiny and influence. It is as if we have said to our children, "Sow your wild oats while you are in college. Soon you will be in the real world and have responsibilities. You are only young once, enjoy it; God can't see you." There can be serious repercussions to sending children to college with the idea they are hidden from God. Not only can children be called to judgment unprepared (college students are uniquely susceptible to sudden death through automobile accidents and violence), but they will face more immoral and harmful influence in college if they wander from God's protection.

COLLEGE MAY NOT BE SAFE

Parents dream of college as a place where their children can safely evolve from adolescence to adulthood. They assume or hope college will buffer them from the full dangers of the adult world. Parents often have an idealized notion college will provide structure, supervision, and guidance. In reality, today's colleges are seldom a safe haven for children. There are no curfews, no signing out of the dormitories and no regulation of overnight guests in the dorm. Lack of supervision, easy access to alcohol, drugs and plenty of free time create an opportune climate for risky and dangerous behavior.

Parents should not count on college professors to provide positive influence and guidance. For example, a college freshman said the topic the English professor gave for his class paper was, "If a film featured a woman sticking needles in men's testicles, would it be a box office success?

Why?" The risks for teenagers, which preoccupied their parents during their children's high school years, do not disappear when they enter college; they sometimes become worse.

Most colleges today avoid creating an environment that protects immature students from their poor choices. To the contrary, colleges, having experienced the over involvement of some parents (labeled "helicopter parents"), may go to considerable lengths to create an environment that supports the myth that college students are responsible adults.

For example, it seems to me that a college refusing access of the parents to their child's academic performance is unreasonable.

Going to college will change the parent/child relationship. There is no way parents can, or should, treat their college age children the way they did when the children lived at home. However, if parents want their children to maintain a value system similar to the one they had before college, the parents need to tell them what they expect. The parents should verbalize what they expect of their college student in regard to use of alcohol and drugs, sexual promiscuity, study time and church attendance. Teenagers are very concrete in their thinking. If not told what their parents expect, many conclude the parents are covertly giving him/her permission to disregard all rules the parents had when the child lived at home.

Parents may need to continue to shoulder some responsibility for their college-age child's behavior, safety, morality and religious life. It is helpful if young students have the continued positive influence of their parents to bolster them as they move into the extended adolescence of college.

Why do we put our heads in the sand and turn our backs on our children just because they go to college? One common reason is that parents are tired of the hassle and responsibility of raising children and feel they deserve a rest. I have seen few parents exhibit the empty nest syndrome (parents becoming depressed when their children leave home). Most parents are ready for their children to be out of the home and for the children to make their own decisions.

Letting college freshmen have complete control of whether they will study, drink alcohol, use drugs, get enough sleep, eat healthy foods, be sexually active, go to class and attend church is similar to leaving elementary students unsupervised in a candy store and telling them to decide what their diet will be. Not knowing what their children are doing, often gives parents a false sense of security. Sometimes this can be a dangerous delusion.

Some parents, early in their child's life, permitted nannies, teachers, television and social pressure to be primarily responsible for child rearing. It is not surprising these parents are also quick to give college the responsibility of finishing their last stage of parenting.

Strangely, other parents may not feel they have a right to make demands on their children once they leave for college. A closer look at this interaction will reveal this is not a new pattern between parent and child. Usually, long before their children's college stage, these parents had given up much of their power to their children. Examples are timid parents who are afraid to go into their child's room because the child will accuse them of "invading his or her privacy." Parents who have so little power and respect from their children will have much less influence on how their children will conduct themselves in college.

ISN'T KNOWLEDGE THE POINT?

When parents send their children to college, they may over-emphasize the importance of children having a good time. Social life may be presented as the focal point of the student's life. Parents may encourage their children to join fraternities and sororities without knowing whether the group's behavior contradicts the values the parents have taught.

Parents hear of drunken escapades and wild parties and then joke with their children about their hangovers. We may dismiss such behavior as harmless, as we ourselves had similar experiences and survived them. Such an attitude does not offer adequate protection for our children. Today's environment is more perilous. Drugs are readily available to augment or replace alcohol. Students now talk of their "drug of choice" which includes alcohol, marijuana, cocaine, speed or hallucinogens. The moral fiber of our adolescents has weakened. Aggressive and sexual behavior is less controlled. What once was drunken revelry now becomes costly vandalism; what used to end in a bloody nose now may result in a fatal beating, stabbing, shooting or gang assault; what in days past may have ended with a slap can now become date or gang rape; and what once was a worry about reputation has progressed to the impact of having an abortion, herpes or AIDS.

STUDY REQUIREMENTS

Parents often make great sacrifices to send a child to college. Is it unreasonable for parents to tell their children they are sending them to college on the condition they attend class and sleep each night in their dorm or apartment that the parents provide for them? Is it harsh for parents to tell them that drunken escapades are unacceptable? Is a parent out of line to occasionally call their child on Saturday morning to check on whether he or she is hung-over or came in the night before?

Students should understand that, although partying in college may be intense and seem to be the norm, they must achieve good grades, or they may find themselves no more employable than if they had not attended college. A greater number of high school students are going to college. A college degree is no longer assurance a graduate will find a job.

Criteria that employers use to select graduating college students for jobs have become more standardized. Objective criteria, grades and test scores, are used for comparing students. Businesses may only interview students who maintain a high grade point average. Who you know and the fraternity you pledged have become less relevant. If college students are not academically competitive, parents might consider withdrawing them from college until they are more mature, better motivated, and self-disciplined. Spending four years accumulating a low grade point average can be a liability that is difficult to overcome.

Is it realistic to send children to college without conditions and requirements? Where will they ever find a situation where they are given lodging, board, an automobile, gas, car insurance, spending money, a country club (fraternity/sorority) and education with the only stated expectation that they "make the most of the opportunity?" The irresponsible lifestyle some parents provide for college students may make it more difficult for them and the parents when their children try to adjust to the real world once they leave college.

It might be useful for parent and child to view college like a job. Would it be unreasonable for a parent to require the student to work (class + study time) a seven-hour day? Try this calculation: Divide the expense of a semester of college by the number of hours your student is in class or studying. It might surprise you how much you are paying your child.

Many college freshmen can still benefit from a parent's advice about study time. The recommended college load (fifteen hours) is only three hours in class a day. Students coming from packed days of class and extracurricular activities in high school often are bewildered by the amount of free time they have in college and may drift aimlessly. Giving a college freshman study expectations may be helpful.

REQUIRING CHURCH ATTENDANCE

Does your college student go to church? I have four biological children and two stepchildren who have gone to college. I have looked at more college dormitories, found more off-campus apartments and attended more fraternity and sorority homecoming brunches on more college campuses than most fathers. It is embarrassing to admit that, until the senior year of our last college child, I had never attended a church service at a college any of our children were attending. When we looked for college housing, we never considered the location of the most convenient church. We unintentionally were conveying the message to that attending church was so unimportant, it wasn't even worth mentioning.

Some parents say college is an opportunity for their children to sort out their true feelings about religion and to make their own choice. When a child is nursing a hangover on Sunday morning, it is not a deep philosophical religious struggle that is keeping him/her from going to church. If they want to ponder the merits of religion, what is wrong with them doing it on their own time after parents do not support them? I feel obligatory church attendance is the most innocuous, but possibly the most helpful, condition a parent could make on their college-bound child. Can you imagine the positive effect on college students if they went to church every Sunday morning? For one thing, it would influence how late they stayed out and what they did on Saturday night. This in itself might save their lives.

Parents may argue such an approach is not practical. Recently, a father who heard me comment about making church attendance a requirement for going to college asked, "How can you know whether they attend? Aren't you setting up a rule you can not enforce?" It is true if children have been raised without religious influence, it will be difficult to make them go to church when they are at college. On the other hand, the father's question demonstrates how ready parents are to give up the little control they have. Although some might consider it unreasonable, it certainly is within the parents' power to not send their children to college unless they agree to go to church.

If parents decide church attendance is required at college, one strategy for checking compliance might be setting a routine of the parents calling the child each Sunday after the parents return from church. Parents and child could compare and discuss their respective sermons. This is not cruel and unusual punishment!

Parents may be surprised that it improves communication. College students sometimes are difficult to engage in conversation. Questions such as, "What have you been doing? How are your classes? What did you do last night?" are regarded by the student as inane and nosy. It may be a relief to both of you to be able to talk about religion. Another positive strategy is to periodically make a college visit and accompany your children to their church.

What should parents do if their college child regularly defies them? If the parent has provided clear, realistic expectations and conditions for going to college and the child regularly does not meet them, the parent should stop paying for college. This is not a profound or novel suggestion. Three thousand years ago, Solomon said something similar, "Proverbs 17:16, ***Of what use is money in the hand of a fool, since he has no desire to get wisdom?***" If students understand irresponsible conduct and insufficient study time could cause their parents to stop paying for their college education, it should cause them to improve their performance.

The degree of parental involvement a college student will need depends on the maturity of the teen and the college he or she attends. If parents recognize their children's need for a more structured setting, they can direct them to colleges where student activity is better regulated. Some parental control and influence is possible, if parents decide to try. There is nothing wrong with a parent continuing to act like a parent if their dependent student continues to act like a child. When children enter college, the parents' responsibility for their children's behavior is largely completed, but it is not over. College children will not need the intensity of parental involvement they required in high school, but most will need some guidance.

A PARENT/STUDENT CONTRACT

There are parents who practice what I am preaching. The following is an actual contract Marcille and Bonham Magness had their son, Mark, sign before he entered Baylor University in 1981. With the Magness' permission, I have reprinted it multiple times in various publications and presentations over the years. Despite it being considered "old fashioned" or "out of touch" by more modern parents, its value is confirmed by the result. Mark, now Dr. Mark Magness, gratefully acknowledges its contribution to his success as a father and an orthodontist. He asks me to continued to display the contract hoping that it will guide other parents to take a similar path.

RULES AND WORDS OF WISDOM
FOR OUR SON MARC BONHAM MAGNESS
From your loving parents:

1. Your education at college is far more important than any girl or fraternity.
2. It is better to fail on an exam than to cheat on it and pass.
3. Conduct yourself on every date and social function as if your mother and God were right beside you.
4. You may not get married while you are in college.
5. Always be kind and considerate of others, especially your roommates.
6. Do not procrastinate, especially when it involves homework.
7. An average grade is one that is not good enough.
8. On Sundays, you must attend church or Sunday School unless you are ill.

9. Remember, no problem is too great for God to handle, no sin too great to be forgiven.
10. Your parents are the next best thing to God on earth. They love you deeply and want only the best in life for you. Your parents are forgiving.
11. Last but not least, if you follow all the above advice, but forget your relationship with God through Jesus Christ, then nothing else really matters.

When college students come home for vacation, they should reintegrate themselves to their families' routines. Parents should expect their children to eat some meals with the family, come home at a reasonable hour, not trash their room and to attend church with the family. Parents should not tolerate behavior that is inconsiderate, a bad influence on siblings, immoral or disrespectful. For college-age children, home need not be as much fun as being on their own. If it is, children may never decide to leave home.

A comfort and compensation for losing direct control of protecting children when they are away in college can be increasing parental prayer.

CHAPTER TEN

PARENT PRAYING

Prayer nourishes our relationship with God. Using the many attributes of Jesus as our model allows considerable free choice. A strong prayer life is helpful in choosing the best path.

Since becoming a Christian, I have tried various techniques to pray in a way that might be most acceptable to God. I certainly am not a perfect example to follow, but my effort may streamline how you decide what is best for you. The most essential factor is to remember that we have an intermediary. All prayers end with a statement, "In Christ's name I pray."

The hints that follow are what I use for private, silent prayer. They also can be used for public prayer. If asked to pray publicly, I prefer to pray spontaneously. Unrehearsed prayers seem more heartfelt and powerful.

THE LORD'S PRAYER

There is a place in the Bible where Jesus gives specific instruction on how to pray. The night before He was crucified, Jesus explained to the disciples (Matthew 6:9) what is commonly known as the "Lord's Prayer." Some people memorize the Lord's Prayer and recite it as the body or the introduction to more specific prayer requests. Jesus, in Matthew 6:9-13, said, ***"This, then, is how you should pray:***

"'Our Father in heaven, hallowed be your name, your kingdom come, your will be done on earth as it is in heaven. Give us today our daily bread. Forgive us our debts, as we also have forgiven our debtors. And lead us not into temptation, but deliver us from the evil one. For

yours is the kingdom and the power and the glory forever." Amen.

THE ACTS MNEMONIC

The "ACTS method prioritizes praying similarly to the format Christ recommends in the Lord's Prayer.

Adoration – Stating our praise, respect, love for God.
Confession – of our sinfulness.
Thanksgiving – for our many blessing.
Supplication – our prayer requests.

Useing the ACTS mnemonic, when I get to "Supplication, I switch into the "Hand Prayer Guide" described below:

THE HAND PRAYER GUIDE

"**Supplication**" lists pray requests from most important to least important.
Thumb – the closest digit, reminds me to pray for, family and close friends.
Index finger – The finger, used to point when teaching, reminds me to pray for ministers and Church.
Middle finger – The tallest, reminds me to pray for our government leaders.
Ring finger – the weakest of the fingers. encourages me to pray for those who are in poor health.
Little Finger – This is prayer for what I think I need. It comes last.

It helps me to say a silent prayer for anyone I am about to criticize, or to whom I am about to recount an unfortunate or negative story. This often will change my attitude into one that is positive and hopeful toward that person. I begin to look for ways they are improving rather than things that confirm my negative judgements. Such silent prayers are great for defusing anger.

Sometimes I argue with God, giving my reasons it is so important that He heal a friend or relative. The prayers of King David whom God called "***a man after my own heart***" supports this position (1 Samuel 13:24). Recently, I have been adding a new twist in praying for the ill. The Gospels of Matthew, Mark, and Luke report how Jesus first forgave a paralyzed man of his sin, then told him to pick up his mat and walk. Maybe I should first state my recognition of the priority of the soul. I now begin by praying for the person's faith, followed by the prayer for healing. It makes the prayer feel stronger.

My friend, Foster Poole, recently passed away. For thirty-five years he had opened our weekly Bible study with a prayer consisting only of "thanksgiving" to God. In remembrance and tribute to Foster, I have begun devoting one day of the week, I selected Saturday, when all my prayers would express "thanks" to God. Doing this makes my attitude and thoughts more positive and hopeful during the rest of the week. Jesus said we need the faith of a child to enter into Heaven. The first prayer I can remember, a child's prayer, has a "soul" emphasis.

"Now I lay me down to sleep.
I pray the Lord my soul to keep.
If I should die before I wake;
I pray the Lord, my soul to take."

Eighty years later, I have come to realize I may have had it right the first time.

PART II - SUMMING UP

In a nutshell, the answer to childrearing is to love one's children, use good common sense and be guided by the Bible, not worldly standards. "Do as I say and not as I do" is not sufficient; strive be the person you would like your children to become.

- Steep your children in the wisdom of the Ten Commandments. They are a prerequisite for moving into the lessons of the New Testament.
    - Don't ignore Commandments I through IV. They assure your family will put God first, and that your children will obey commandment V.
    - Commandment V, "Honor your father and mother and you will have a long and good life," offers the greatest hope that your children will be successful on earth. It is the basis for respect of authority. "Honor' is more than obedience, it includes attitude.
- Socialize with others with like values, participate in Church activities.
- Don't be a bottom-line parent. Give children credit for sincere intent and effort.
- Encourage your children to serve others. This plants the seed of the Fruit of the Spirit.
- Remember that the goal of parenting is not to provide a successful childhood, but to grow your child into an adult who is a good person. The ultimate example of a good person is Jesus Christ.
- Be cautious about sleepovers.
- Appreciate the seriousness of drug and alcohol use. Guard your children from them.

- Make attending church a condition for attending college, and be explicit about your expectations for the student's behavior.
- Remember these words from Jesus:

"Take my yoke upon you and learn from me, for I am gentle and humble in heart, and you will find rest for your souls. For my yoke is easy and my burden is light." Matthew 11:29-30.

NOTES

1. "The effects of Mother Child Separation: A Follow-up Study," British Journal of Medical Psychology, 29:211, 1956.

2. "The Nature of Love," American Psychologist, 13:673, 1958.

3. "Hospitalism: An Inquiry into the Genesis of Psychiatric Conditions in Early Childhood," in Eisler, R.S., et al. (Eds.), The Psychoanalytic Study of the Child, International Universities Press, vol. 1, pp. 53-74, New York, 1945.

4. Dobson, Dr. James; The New Dare to Discipline, Tyndal House Publishers, Inc., 1990.

5. Ron Cresswell, attorney, Johnson Johnson Cresswell Monk, PC Dallas, Texas.

www.ingramcontent.com/pod-product-compliance
Lightning Source LLC
Chambersburg PA
CBHW020931090426
42736CB00010B/1109